P9-DDS-841

The
Wreckage
of My
Presence

The Wreckage of My Presence

ESSAYS

Casey Wilson

HARPER

An Imprint of HarperCollins*Publishers*

THE WRECKAGE OF MY PRESENCE. Copyright © 2021 by Casey Wilson. All rights reserved. Printed in the United States of America. No part of this book may be used or reproduced in any manner whatsoever without written permission except in the case of brief quotations embodied in critical articles and reviews. For information, address HarperCollins Publishers, 195 Broadway, New York, NY 10007.

HarperCollins books may be purchased for educational, business, or sales promotional use. For information, please email the Special Markets Department at SPsales@harpercollins.com.

FIRST EDITION

Designed by Elina Cohen

Library of Congress Cataloging-in-Publication Data has been applied for.

ISBN 978-0-06-296058-0

21 22 23 24 25 LSC 10 9 8 7 6 5 4 3

FOR MY BROTHER, FLETCHER

CONTENTS

AUTHOR'S NOTE

The events in this book are all true and retold to the best of my recollection. While the spirit and tone of the dialogue is as it occurred, it is not word for word. Some names, identifying circumstances, and details have been changed in order to protect the privacy of the various individuals involved.

The Wreckage of My Presence

Bed Person

I am a bed person.

When my husband and I were buying furniture for our new house and weighing various options, my questions were always, "Could the couch be deeper? Could we add an L to that? Could it be a chaise? Could the chairs recline like a JetBlue Mint seat?" My husband finally stopped me and said that in a perfect world, I'd want every piece of furniture to be a California king and our house would resemble a meth den. He tells people that if I could I'd walk around with two mattresses strapped to my front and back so I could flop down at any moment.

He's not wrong. And this is because, I'm a bed person. It's a label I'm alarmingly comfortable with—maybe too comfortable—and one I consider both a state of mind and a way of being.

A bed person is someone who wants to recline at all times. When lying down is not an option, we will find a way to remain seated, preferably at an angle, and if we have to stand you will never not find us in a *deep* lean.

I'll stretch out anywhere. If I'm out for drinks, I'll hunch over the bar with my face almost grazing the wood.

At parties I'll dance from my stool, waist up, going *after it* but too tired to get vertical and bring my moves to the dance floor. I favor Pilates classes that let me work out while lying down on a Reformer. I meditate lying down because doing it seated feels like an assault on my skeleton. I prefer movie theaters where I can pay double for the privilege of reclining in the seat so that, if the movie is bad, I have the option to sleep. (Let's be honest, I'm really going for the candy and a nap. And the two go hand in hand, because if you buy enough concessions, they'll shut down your system when the freight of sugar hits your bloodstream.) One of my key criteria for judging a movie is: Is it too loud to sleep through? I hate when directors don't take into consideration that some of us might only be watching in order to *not* watch and, in fact, sleep. When will movie studios keep my brethren and me in mind and make the proper aural accommodations?!

And when I'm in front of the camera and we're blocking out the choreography of a scene, you bet your sweet tush I'm pitching for the character to take a load off, no matter the setting or situation. As I'm sure Meryl Streep and all the greats do.

For such an energetic person, the truth is I'm so very tired. Maybe it's my medication, maybe it's my Taurus moon, or, as I like to tell myself, maybe it's because I give *so* very much. This truth is disturbing to parent-friends who often ask, "Can you stay awake during this play-date?" Not really, no. I want to respond, "Could YOU try and keep me awake with a tidbit of conversation that contains one iota, one kernel of hot goss? SOMETHING ONE MIGHT WANT TO STAY AWAKE *FOR*??" Keeping me awake is as much the other person's job as it is mine. If you spy me catching some winks and long blinks, that's on you.

I once read an article about famed Hollywood super-agent Sue Mengers and how she did *everything* from bed: took meetings from bed, received friends in bed, hosted parties from bed, and ate, smoked, and drank in bed— all while wearing a caftan and oversize sunglasses. Her image has been cut out and pasted on the vision board of my dreams.

Like Sue, my husband, David, and I eat many of our meals (*definitely* all our dinners) in bed. I'm dismayed to report that we've taken to silently unfolding a large beach towel and placing it over our white duvet before digging in. We keep small salt and pepper shakers on our nightstands at all times, and a ketchup bottle often lives there as well. This horrifies some of our friends. "Wait, you mean you eat the occasional postdinner snack in bed . . . ?" they ask hopefully.

I have to break it to them. "No . . . we'll cut into a chicken Parm or a filet in bed."

"Once in a while??" they plead. "Only on the weekends?"

"No. Every night."

We have two children under the age of six, and by the time we feed them and get them to sleep it's all we can do to collapse into bed with our dinner. On a really ambitious night, one of us will throw our take-out boxes just outside our bedroom door, as though we think a room service captain will be trawling our halls to clear empty trays.

I am also a bath person. Most bed people are. Bed people and bath people go together like Dr Pepper and Goobers.

Nonbath people don't get it. They're always saying inane things like, "Don't you feel like you're just sitting in your own filth??" Or, "Don't you get bored in there?" I want to ask, "Did YOU get bored in the womb?"

From a purely organizational standpoint, most people underestimate the amount of multitasking you can do in a tub. Being submerged in water doesn't have to limit your productivity a bit. I can read, or take calls, and when good friends come over, I have no problem asking them if we can take things to the tub. Ever the hostess, I'll pull out a tiny pop-up seat, the kind I use on the rare occasion when my sons are in the bath and I'm not in it with them, and my friends and I will chat away. If anything, I think I could be doing *more* in there. My friend June strips down, pops in her earbuds, and does her therapy from the bath. I read that actress Rachel Bloom uses a caddy to hold her laptop so she can *work* from the bath. I salute these trailblazers.

If you haven't guessed, I never rely on bubbles to cover me for modesty, and I think this type of behavior goes hand in hand with someone who prances about a locker room nude. Which I do. It's not that I think I look so good—God no—it's that I can't be bothered to care at all. Which can be problematic. After the births of both of my kids, I spirited away tons of pairs of the mesh undies Cedars-Sinai offers up to new mothers. I wore them *long* after I needed them. They were comfortable! They made me feel held and safe. To ease the transition back into my sexy nude sports thongs, I took a pit stop in *enormous* nude-colored Hanes briefs that went up past my belly button. I WANTED TO BE COMFORTABLE!!

(A word on nude panties in general: while I don't normally care about what men want in the bedroom, I will advise THEY DON'T LIKE NUDE UNDIES. Nude is not an alluring color. And while we're circling the drain on this one, though my husband would most likely prefer me to wax even a skosh—never asked him!—the one time I did, it was so painful that I left halfway through the procedure with one side done, one side . . . unkempt. David is a very attractive man, and the thought seizes me every so often in the middle of the night that I should maybe step it up. It's usually when I am wearing my favorite nightshirt, an oversize, off-the-shoulder Adele T-shirt I got at her concert. David says it most likely only came in one size: eating-ice-cream-and-crying size. The perfect size. I wear it proudly while doing both those things, and I like to imagine my fellow sisters across the globe wearing theirs, too.)

One is not born a bed or bath person. Though genetics clearly play a role, I believe it's learned behavior. When I was in middle school, on Fridays my mom would pick up my girlfriends and me from school and drive us straight to

7–Eleven. She allowed us to buy as much candy and soda as we wanted from Sev Lev, provided she didn't have to get out of the car. Then we'd head to Blockbuster and rent a movie (usually *Terms of Endearment*), go to our house, immediately order Domino's and then run upstairs and all get into my parents' waterbed. Together. This lasted until tenth, eleventh grade. None of my girlfriends found this odd, or if they did, they politely never said anything.

In the waterbed we'd play "Girlfriends," a game that consisted of my mom talking to us in a baby voice and us responding in kind. It's a hard voice to convey through the written word, so if you are so inclined, I'd like to offer you the opportunity to hear me do it in a recording. Simply visit: hc.com/caseywilson.

It's specific, isn't it?! We would all speak to each other in this voice. It was as natural as eating six slices of Domino's and washing them down with three Cherry Cokes. Most of my mom's monologues devolved into ramblings about our beagle, Josie. "All da girlfriends are here but we can't forget about da odder girlfriend. Da beagie baby Josie, who wants to also be da girlfriend. We can't leave the beagie baby out. She da girlfriend too and da president of da Beagie Society." Shortly after completing this performance, my mom would *abruptly* fall asleep, and my girlfriends and I would continue watching the movie with Josie at our feet, swaying up and down on the high seas of my parents' waterbed until my dad came home from work. I would sometimes hear my brother pass the

open door with a friend and explain casually, "My mom
and my sister and her friends are playing Girlfriends."

Given their love of their bed, it was a surprise when
my parents decided to start sleeping on the pull-out couch
in our den. Immediately upon entering the house you'd
be treated to a full view of my parents' new "bedroom."
And, often, the two of them, snuggled under the covers
watching TV. They'd wave brightly, with a "Pretend we're
not here!" Their rationale for the move was officially that
Josie couldn't handle the stairs to their original bedroom
very well anymore, but I think the real reason was that
my *mom* didn't feel like climbing the stairs anymore.

Once she and my dad set themselves up in the den,
things got stranger and stranger by the day. Whenever
anyone came in, Mom would brag about her ingenuity:

"Look! I got some Velcro at Safeway and stuck the
two remotes together so it's one big double-sided remote!
I don't know why no one's ever thought of this! We never
lose it!" or "We started just keeping the pull-out couch
unfolded permanently so we never have to deal with closing it and reopening it!" or, gesturing to our fire poker,
"Look where I hang my nightie!"

If my mother was a bed person, my father was . . . a
bath person. He was NEVER NOT TAKING A BATH
OR ABOUT TO TAKE A BATH OR GETTING OUT OF A
BATH. When my parents would host a party and the doorbell signaled the arrival of the first guests, that's when
he would turn the bath *on*. Our house wasn't that big, so

the guests would hear the water running, and I'd have to tell them the truth. "My dad'll be right down, seems he's just gotten into . . . the bath." It was unusual. Before my grandma's funeral, we were all dressed up and standing under the carport outside her house, ready to get into my grandfather's Lincoln Town Car, when we heard the telltale rumble of the pipes. "JESUS CHRIST, PAUL!!" my grandfather screamed at his son-in-law.

Paul Wilson also loves a hot tub—or, as he calls it, a "talk tub," since he sets the temperature to a more reasonable degree, which he feels encourages people to linger and chat. He's never happier than when he's shoulder to shoulder with friends and strangers alike in a lukewarm hot tub, "connecting."

But he doesn't need company to get his fix. He bought a small aboveground hot tub right after my mom died, the way some men get a flashy red sports car after a divorce. It has LED lights that strobe in time to the music coming from the built-in speakers. EVERY SINGLE MORNING my dad goes "tubbin'." He sits outside, rain or shine, with a cigar and the *Washington Post,* and rolls his calls through to the tub. He talks LOUDLY. So loudly, in fact, that the neighbors on both sides built fences around their houses and added mature hedges so the sight of my dad didn't greet them at the start of each day like a suburban rooster.

A bed person and a bath person raised a child in their own image, one who would develop her own womb-like defenses against the harsh world.

I am an adult thumb sucker. It's not great, I know. I guess it's rather astonishing that at thirty-nine I have yet to stop. No one can believe I suck my thumb around my husband, but he says at this point it would be odd if I didn't. Old friends claim they "don't even see it anymore." That's how natural it has become. BUT *SHOULD* IT BE SO NORMALIZED??? Again, I blame them all for making me feel so free to be me.

It was a real wake-up call when our pediatrician instructed me to get rid of my older son's pacifier, saying it was, simply, "time." My son was three. I was horrified. I was being made to ask my son to do something I could not, nor could ever, do?! Forcing him to cross an emotional threshold and part with a comfort so deep it made my eyes well up with tears just thinking about it? I debated with him. "But, I mean, who are we to be the arbiters of when it's time for anyone to give up something?? How can we know??" The doctor looked at me. "Well, you're his mom, that's who. And pediatricians, dentists, and child psychologists all agree that *this* is the time." I nodded. "Hmm."

When he wailed for them that first night, I wailed along with him; he was going through something I could not fathom. I never even tried to give it up. And at three, he succeeded. He is stronger than me, easily. Both of my kids are.

I have been in analysis for fourteen years, and David *often* asks me what Dr. Myers thinks about my thumb. Has it come up? "Of course it has, and she doesn't seem that bothered by it," I say. I follow up with my standard retort when forced to defend this practice: "It's better than drugs!" When this doesn't assuage him, I confide the real truth: "Honestly, I think Dr. Myers is just more worried about other things with me." David nods vigorously. "Yeah, yeah, okay, that makes sense. Little more chicken left on that bone. For *sure*."

What it comes down to is this. I am simply a person of comfort and excess. As my dear friend Kulap says, "You refuse to apologize for living a celebratory life." Hear! Hear! And while we're at it, you may have guessed that I also love Ambien; NyQuil (none of this melatonin shit); wine; tequila; piña coladas; margaritas (vodka is for people who want to punish themselves); CBD gummies (I'm solely there for the gummy); a rogue pill a friend has left over after a surgery; half-and-half with a splash of coffee, two Splenda, and three pumps of peppermint; candy; Cinnabon; Wetzel's Pretzels; Annie's Pretzels; furry slippers and fuzzy robes; trashy magazines; garbage television; unconfirmed gossip; spas; lasers; luxury; healers of all stripes; extravagant gifts; surprise parties; choreographed dances with friends at any age; karaoke; musicals; Christmas decorations that include a "table tree;" naps; joining gyms I will never go to; hiring trainers I pay up front and then never go to; starting radical diets I never follow through on . . . I overspend, I overeat, I overdo.

And I know it's just a matter of time until David and I move our bed into the living room.

The Wreckage
of My Presence

The spring of 2002 found me fresh out of NYU with a theater degree and an unfulfilled women's studies minor. Ready to take on the world! I wasn't too worried that I didn't have a job because I was 100 percent sure fame of epic proportion was just around the corner. A celebrity so debilitating I felt I should savor these last anonymous days. But in the mean and between time I did need money.

I tried waitressing at EJ's Luncheonette, an upscale downtown pancakery, but was fired because of my tendency to address patrons' bad behavior directly. This incident in particular pushed things over the edge. When an incredibly rude and entitled man threw a bunch of pennies on the table as my tip (likely because I was a *wildly* bad waitress), I took that opportunity to shame him in front of his wife and the entire restaurant. "Sir!" I yelled, just as they got to the door. "Actually, no. What I am about to say is meant for your wife. Ma'am. I just had to spend one hour with your husband, but I am so sorry you have to spend a lifetime with him. I wish you luck in this endeavor. You have my sincere condolences."

Over the summer, I got a job performing murder mystery plays in an abandoned crab shack in Kennebunkport, Maine. The actors outnumbered the audience, which isn't ideal. We were all sent home midsummer.

It was back to Craigslist, my entrée into the postcollegiate working world. I responded to a million ads and hoped for the sake of my next employer they had a backup plan for when I was inevitably plucked from the trenches and carried through the streets of Hollywood.

I got a job babysitting for a precocious six-year-old girl, who was smarter than I was, in the way New York City kids tend to be. She had an unsettling habit of vigorously jamming the legs of her Barbie doll in and out of her vagina whenever I left her in the bathtub alone so I could rummage through the kitchen cabinets for her Halloween candy. I was never not DEAD ASLEEP, sprawled out on the couch with the TV blaring and Starburst wrappers littering the floor, when her parents came home from dinner. They would have to shake me awake, which probably didn't inspire much confidence in terms of what kind of get-up-and-go I would display during an emergency. The final straw came after the girl's mother caught *me* vigorously jamming a fork into a toaster to remove her daughter's English muffin. I didn't know the toaster had to be unplugged in order for you to do that. I'm sure her daughter did.

My BFF and roommate, June Diane Raphael, and I

attempted to sell hair-care products over the phone. June bravely made the first call. The man who answered said he had no use for our products because he was bald and to take him off our goddamn list. June threw the phone across the room in a panic, but undeterred, I picked it up and sweetly asked if his wife had any hair.

We had a lot to juggle between our hair-care sales job, rehearsals for our two-woman sketch comedy show, and our internship for one of my all-time favorite actresses, Susan Sarandon. Twice a week we would make our way to her gorgeous office in Union Square and run errands and mail packages and so on. Our "supervisor" was Susan's main assistant, a lovely man who for reasons unknown was in possession of Famke Janssen's dog, who always sat atop his lap while he "rolled calls." My main task was to sit behind him, open Susan's fan mail, and when appropriate, send back a presigned glossy headshot. I say when appropriate because it wasn't always appropriate to send a photo of Susan sexily lounging on a pickup truck in a still from *Bull Durham* when the fan mail was written by a man on death row. Many people on death row wrote to Susan because of her role in *Dead Man Walking*. The letters were absolutely heartbreaking. They would tell their stories and often include photos of themselves or photos of their families. I knew my job as fourth assistant was limited in scope and firm in its parameters, however . . . these letters. They were devastating. I couldn't help but respond. As Susan. First a "Thinking of you!" here, then a "This will all be over soon!" there. Day by day, I became more and more emboldened, and in no time, my Susan started crafting paragraph-long, empathetic responses. I figured this was good for her brand! Fake Susan was also pocketing the change and small bills that often accompanied the letters from suburban women hoping to ensure a headshot would be sent. It was a thrill to see the change tumble out of every tenth envelope. The real Susan didn't need the money, I rationalized.

June and I also rationalized our use of the real Susan's office after hours (again, just here and there!) to print and mail *our* headshots around town. What about our careers?! She'd already made it! Weren't we all just actresses honing our craft and navigating the biz as best we knew how? Upon discovering this, our supervisor politely asked us to turn in our keys and please never return.

Many, many years later I got a part in the wonderful movie *The Meddler* and had two scenes with the real Susan. In my tenure as her assistant's assistant's intern's intern, I'd never met her. I thought long and hard about whether I should mention my stint on her staff when I essentially (but understandably?) committed identify theft. I realized my tracks were sadly covered, since, unfortunately, those who had written the letters were most likely no longer with us. I decided my best course of action was simply to meet Susan anew, under my own steam. As peers. She could not have been more lovely. I regret nothing.

Finally, a steady employment ship sailed into harbor in the form of a very thin, manic, reflexive documentary filmmaker named Barbara Monette, who'd never made one film. She "needed" a personal assistant five days a week and was paying A LOTTTTTTT. $20/hour. Jackpot.

"So tell me about Susan." These were Barbara's first words to me during my interview. I had, of course, ever so slightly embellished my role in Susan's company on my résumé. And as luck would have it, Barbara was *the* most blatant starfucker I have ever encountered, before or since! I was hired on the spot. That should've been the first red flag. I witnessed approximately a gazillion others during the first twenty minutes of the interview, like when she asked if I would be comfortable "cheering her on" via speakerphone while she ran on the treadmill at Equinox. Or when she said casually, "I just left my husband. I'm a late-in-life lesbian as of six months ago. He's devastated. He's right over there," as she pointed to the desk DIRECTLY NEXT TO US, where an older, clearly beaten-down man wearing headphones was working. "He funds all my docs. Well, the ones I'm working on getting made."

But red flags have never deterred me! I brushed aside my concerns and accepted the position. I would be working in a cool loft-like space in the West Village where on one side of the office about six employees seemed to be working on real, revenue-generating projects having to do with computers and graphics, and the other side of the office was myself and Barbara, working on her vision board.

IT BECAME IMMEDIATELY clear to me that Barbara had an issue with food. I wouldn't see her eat anything for days at a time. She would drink six cups of coffee which made her jittery and aggressive. I would have felt badly for her if she wasn't so mean. She regularly accused me of stealing, and while I just mentioned I stole someone's office space, I genuinely would never steal money. Except, I guess, for the change I mentioned earlier. She would pace and ramble around the office, her lower jaw jutting in and out almost violently when she talked. This is when she would come in at all. She found me dim, and I don't blame her; I can't say I was the most motivated employee. By this time, June and I had begun performing our two-woman show, which we'd named *Rode Hard and Put Away Wet* (based on a phrase my mom used for a woman who had too many miles on her) at the Upright Citizens Brigade Theatre. I was up to my old tricks again, brazenly running the promotional campaign for it out of Barbara's office. Barbara was *always* finding flyers I'd left in the copier, hot pink 8.5-by-11s with an image of June and me splayed out sexily in a Manhattan street and licking lollipops. The caption read: "Sketch comedy by girls who aren't ugly!" (As you can imagine, we ingratiated ourselves *immediately* with the women at the theater. Just kidding! They hated us. To be clear, none of them were ugly, we had never even met any of them; this was just our attempt to highlight and challenge the inherent misogyny of the sketch world. No one saw it that way. So that was a misstep.) I also answered Barbara's phone, so it felt only fair that the number should double as the reservations line for our show. To whom much is given much is required. What was the big?

Speaking of big . . . . Barbara was, as many people with eating disorders are, obsessed with *my* weight. Skinny I was not. But not overweight either. I was cute enough and just couldn't get it up to care about a few extra lbs. My passivity surrounding my body seemed to ENRAGE Barbara, though. INFURIATE her. She'd peek between the crack in the walls that separated our cubicles when I returned from my daily trip to Balthazar with a focaccia sandwich, giant cookie, and a can of Coca-Cola she paid for. You heard me. I didn't even have the self-respect or dignity to get a Diet Coke. I think I'm the only actress in history who has ever tasted The Real Thing.

One day she asked me to come into her office because she wanted to talk about "all this." She gestured up and down my frame.

ME: Come again?

BARBARA: I'd like to offer you a gift. I'd like for you to leave the office immediately—

ME: For a paid personal day?!

BARBARA: And attend a 12-step program meeting in the Village.

ME: I'm sorry?

BARBARA: For food addiction.

ME: But I don't think I sdkndnfihfdi???

BARBARA: Please swallow your focaccia bread before you speak. It's a wonderful program for people like you who binge-eat and struggle with or obsess over food. Or under-eat, although that doesn't seem to be your . . . affliction.

She looked at her computer.

BARBARA: Tom D. is leading today's meeting in the basement of a church next door to Bobst Library at NYU. He's excellent. Used to put on diapers so he wouldn't have to stop eating when he needed to shit and now he looks terrific. I'll pay you for the hour if you'll just go. You want to be an actress and I'm telling you, it won't work out for you if you don't go.

Long pause.

ME (*brightly*): Great!

And off I went. To grab a vanilla Frappuccino with whip and a blueberry scone from Starbucks (one of the great baked goods America has to offer. STARBUCKS IS AN UNDERRATED BAKERY!!!).

I wasn't hurt by Barbara's words so much as confused. I loved food, sure. I just wasn't quite sure I had a problem with food, per se, beyond loving it so.

After all, I'd seen this particular problem close-up.

My mom struggled with her weight, most of the struggle being in her mind and it was painful to watch. Many a time she'd collapse after coming home from her full-time job as director of a preschool in our town and wrapping up her second gig as Kathy "I'll Do Anything for My Daughter" Wilson (as my friends embarrassingly but accurately dubbed her). She would settle in and order two large pizzas, then polish them off with two bags of Pepperidge Farm Mint Milanos and her own liter of The Real Thing. Afterward, she'd fall into what seemed to be a food coma in the den/bedroom. Every month or so, things got darker and she would retreat to her original bedroom/den for a few days at a time. Then she would be back full steam and raring to go. I was never really sure what was going on, but it didn't seem . . . healthy?

That said, however unbothered I was by my own attitude toward food, I pretended to go to meetings for the entire year I worked with Barbara. It became an amazing excuse to run out midday for a great audition, like a Zelnorm bloated stomach campaign. (BOOKED IT!!!!!! Much like Carrie from *Sex and the City*, my stomach was on a bus!)

Barbara would periodically ask me how it was going, how my sponsor (Linda R., entirely made up) and I were gelling. "GREAT," I'd assure her. "Linda is there for me day or night. She was really in the food this week."

One day, when I was near the twelve-month mark with Barbara, I felt a quarter hit my head and realized she wanted to see me. (She'd routinely throw pennies at my head when she needed me and either of us was on the phone. It would drive her crazy when I wouldn't realize the source of the pennies, and put them in my desk or purse, assuming they fell from heaven. Incensed, she'd graduated to bigger change—a dime here, a nickel there.)

I entered Barbara's cubicle and found her in tears. She told me her ex-husband was evicting her (us) from the office, effective immediately. He had finally had it with her and with funding her whims. Barbara was livid. How could he expect her to leave *now*??? She had JUST come back from a three-week research trip to France, where she'd stayed at the Four Seasons to feel the energy of Truffaut and tinkered with a first draft of an erotic short film she was thinking about possibly toying with the idea of shooting with his money. "This is outrageous," I reassured her. "One cannot disrupt an artist at work."

Her ex-husband was working in London with his entire team for the next two weeks, but he wanted us gone by the end of the day. This worried me, because I had a 12-step meeting (Aveda hair show audition) at noon.

She told me that her ex had called the super and the building manager, and they'd be arriving at five to make sure we were out. As she cried I frantically wondered how I'd reroute the RSVPs to my comedy show, then started packing my things.

But Barbara, ever defiant, had a different plan. "We just simply . . . won't leave. No one will be the wiser," she told me, with crazy-eyed resolve. "If we don't open the door, they can't kick us out! We just have to avoid the

super, use the fire escape, and once we're inside, lock the
door. What are they gonna do? Break the door down and
drag us out?"

And so, each morning for the next two weeks, we waited
in the neighboring deli to make sure the super wasn't in
the lobby, then scurried in like little mice. Once inside,
Barbara and I would behave as if it were business as usual,
which for her meant no business at all. While I couldn't
make my normal trips to the NARS counter to hunt down
a new "power red" lipstick for Barbara or scour the city
for obscure protein powders, I could still cold-call acting
agencies to see if Diane Lane would consider lending her
talents for free to a short film where she would have to be
naked from the waist down 80 percent of the time.

They were strange days.

Then one afternoon we heard a knock at the door.
"FedEx!" a guy yelled from the other side. Barbara froze.
Then she did what she would do when anyone came to
the door during this period: she got into the freestanding
wardrobe and hid behind the coats. She whisper-shouted
at me to look through the peephole and answer the door
ONLY if the deliveryman didn't seem suspicious. I'll admit that when I peered out, I saw that he was neither in
uniform nor carrying a package, but I opened it anyway.
He promptly served us with papers.

I'm not quite sure why I opened the door. Maybe it was
just instinctive—I had signed exclusively for non-work-
related packages for Barbara over the year—but maybe it
was a cry for help. A way out.

Either way, the jig was up for Barbara, and for me. She screamed at me for over twenty minutes for opening the door and I let loose a torrent of rage you only dream you will ever get to yell at an abusive boss. I said the kinds of things you nomally kick yourself for *not* saying after the fact. I called her a "creative succubus garbagy talentless fuck." I'd had enough of this unhinged wreck of a human. I got in her face—close enough that I could smell her fortieth cup of coffee—and yelled, "WRITE ME MY LAST CHECK NOW, YOU FUCKING GODDAMN BITCH!!!" It was alarming to both of us. Hands shaking, she wrote out my final check. Then I emptied my desk of all the loose change that had been thrown at my melon and walked out, assuming I'd never see her again. Bridge burned.

Until.

Months and months later, June and I were backstage at the Upright Citizens Brigade Theatre (UCB), changing out of our costumes after one of our last performances of *Rode Hard*. The show had been chosen for the Aspen HBO Comedy Festival, a dream we'd had for it since the very beginning. That festival would ultimately start our careers and solidify a lifelong creative partnership and even deeper friendship between my touchstone, June, and me. It was in Aspen that we met an executive named Heidi Sherman Grey, who tapped us to write a movie for Kate Hudson and Anne Hathaway called *Bride Wars*. After we got over our devastation that someone saw us as writers rather than STARS OF STAGE AND SCREEN, that single job led to more and more and eventually we got our gorgeous mugs in front of the camera. As God intended.

But on this particular night, we were having a laugh as we took off our makeup. We were wearing quite a bit of it because the final sketch had been a fantasy about what would happen if Joan Crawford and Bette Davis met in present day as their characters from *What Ever Happened to Baby Jane?* and started to physically fight each other; June played Joan and I was Bette. (WE WERE THE RYAN MURPHYS OF 2004!)

There was a knock at the door. It was Barbara. What ever happened to baby Barbara, indeed? She had come to the show, alone. Funny, June hadn't gotten her RSVP on the landline of the antique business where she worked, which was now our central headquarters. June may not have known Barbara would be attending even if she had gotten an RSVP, because since I'd last seen her, Barbara had legally changed her last name from Monette to Mon*et*. A former coworker from the legit side of the office told me this was to seem related to the painter Claude Monet and hopefully impress people. Dark stuff.

I was shocked to see her. I had gotten into therapy because of her. Well, not entirely because of her, but because the way she treated me activated events from my past I had been comfortable burying but were now comin' to the old surface as they are wont to do. I also went because I was in my early twenties and, much like Barbara, was also an unhinged wreck of a person. I said hello and thanked her for coming. She had an expression on her face I'd never seen before. She looked awestruck. She looked alive. She looked inspired and . . . friendly.

Barbara grabbed my hand and said, "You are *so* good, Casey." She had tears in her eyes. "You are so talented. I knew it. I just knew you would be and that's why I . . . why I always . . ." She trailed off. I could feel she wanted to say "That's why I wanted you to lose weight." Why she'd pushed me.

I was taken aback. I had spent so much of my post-college life on her life. But now I saw it, as absolutely ass backward as it was: she really believed in me and always had. But I still didn't quite understand why she equated weight loss with success.

But the manager who signed me after The Aspen Comedy Festival echoed Barbara. I needed to lose weight. Not a lot, but enough to look on camera like I looked in real life. I did as I was told, which coincidentally coincided with my beginning to get work as an actress.

In 2007, I auditioned for *Julie & Julia* in the morning for Nora Ephron and for *Saturday Night Live* in the afternoon for Lorne Michaels. I got both jobs. A miracle. But if I'm being honest, I'm not sure if I would have gotten them if I hadn't lost the weight. I'd like to think so. There is a dark adage that floats around *SNL*—you either have to lose weight or gain it to be on the show, but you can't be "in between." In the year and a half of utter madness I was there, still grieving the loss of my mom, I began taking antidepressants to try and lift myself up, but I gained back all the weight I'd lost, and some more, from mainlining Magnolia cupcakes and trying to handle the Barbaras of 30 Rock. (She had prepared me well, in that regard.) When I was not asked back for what would have been my third season, I felt a rush of relief and utter disappointment in myself. I had the chance and I didn't take my shot. But I never cried. The relief outweighed the regret.

However, a week later an article ran in *The Hollywood Reporter* saying that I was fired for being fat. (It was on the CNN ticker, too. My father had to see that. Although it is his favorite source for news . . . it wasn't what you want.) Though it had been a week since I was let go, *that* was the night I cried. I wailed. I've never been more humiliated or felt more exposed. I wanted to hide in my own freestanding wardrobe. The murmurs and directives I had received from managers and bosses alike were one thing, but to hear this on a national scale . . . I was crushed. And angry that my grief over the loss of my mom had contributed to another trauma. I hadn't been able to keep all the balls in the air, and now everyone could see it. That's the thing about weight, it can't be hidden.

I flashed on a scene from my childhood. My brother, Fletcher, and I and a couple of my girlfriends have settled in to watch *Ally McBeal* with my mom. We can't find the remote, but my mom spots it across the room in front of the TV. She has to bend down very low in order to grab it and her pants split. And I laugh. It happens so quickly and is so unexpected. Tears spring to her eyes and she runs upstairs. I follow her and stand helplessly while she wails from the bed, "You laughed at me. You were all laughing at me." I'll never forget the look on her face. I've made peace with most of my regrets, including being let go from *Saturday Night Live*. But not this one.

It occurs to me now that Barbara had been trying to protect me from the world that had been so cruel to her. As a self-loathing woman, she could only act on her urge to love and shelter me by being cruel about my perceived vulnerabilities, which were actually her vulnerabilities. She didn't want me to be sitting in the moment I was currently in. She knew what I didn't yet know, which was that the world is cruel to overweight people.

When people shame you for your size they succeed in reducing you to the smallest version of yourself, emotionally. And I collapsed under that scrutiny. And made a decision. I realized if I wanted to do what I loved—perform and make people laugh—I needed to lose some weight. So I did. But not for them. For me. To protect myself. I chose to become a less visible target in order to shine. (Note: This choice was made because I am on camera. If I were a teacher I would sit my happy ass down, knowing I look FOINE!)

I am a millennial. (An old one, yes. Perhaps the *last* millennial? Born in 1980, I'm on the absolute cusp. Hanging on for dear life. A vintage mill, if you will. And many of my friends won't. To them I say STOP BEING JEAL-OUS.) But as proud as I am of my mill status, I wish to God I were part of the body-positive generation. Lord love 'em. I'm inspired by these young upstarts who celebrate their bodies and don't give a good goddamn fuck what anyone else thinks. I'm so envious. Because I started off that way. In middle school and even high school I had confidence for days. But as I got older, I was swiftly taught by the Barbaras of the world that not only should I not feel confident but I should in fact feel embarrassed about my body. Apologetic. Ashamed of the wreckage I carried around with me. And ever eager to please, I fell in line. Which makes me sad.

But I try to forgive myself. I hope my mom has forgiven me for laughing. As I've forgiven Barbara. And I hope younger women will forgive me. And even younger women will forgive them. And so on. And so forth.

However, five years ago, when Barbara sent me a friend request on Facebook, I hit ignore so hard I almost broke my hand.

To All the Boys
I Loved Before

When we were in our twenties, most of my friends dated bad boys. Mean guys. Assholes they fell in love with after one date because they had yet to work out their daddy issues.

My father was my Girl Scout leader.

And so, I dated . . . good guys. Gentle poets. Guys I met in a yearly play I did in D.C. called *The Christmas Revels*, in which we dressed in old-timey clothes and sang carols while holding lanterns. Soft-spoken, earnest, lovely guys I did not deserve and treated terribly across the board. And there were . . . lots of them.

There was a magician named Ashley.

Three Pauls.

One Deke.

One Turkish waiter.

Tens of improv teachers.

One guy who accidentally farted while we stood at my mom's grave and cried about it in the car the whole way home.

One heir to the Toys R Us Fortune.

One a cappella singer whose specialty was percussion on the J. Geils Band's "[Angel is a] Centerfold."

One balding prop master.

Gays both closeted and out whom I encountered at theater camps across this great nation.

A guy I met after seeing him perform a show for sex ed classes called "How to Love a Rapist." He played the rapist and was a very good actor because in real life, as I problematically told everyone, he "would never rape a fly."

An understudy for Mark in a touring production of *Rent* I met while pretending to be a local journalist who wanted to do a story on him. He broke up with me when he found out I was both not a journalist and, in fact, sixteen.

Jesus of Nazareth in a community theater production of *Jesus Christ Superstar*.

More tens of improv teachers.

And one gun trafficker with a heart of gold.

Before I met my beloved husband, I was an unfortunate combination of boy-crazy and willing to have sex within the first hour of a first date. But to be perfectly honest, it never really backfired on me, because the guys I chose were safe. They were sensitive. They asked permission to kiss . . . surprised me with tickets to the Indigo Girls . . . got their moms to break up with me. Not a one weighed more than 160 pounds sopping wet. I could literally crush them all, and they didn't care; they just wanted to snuggle while listening to Leonard Cohen and DID I MENTION I HAVE MANY REGRETS AND DID NOT DESERVE THEM??? THEY WERE ALL LOVELY, EVEN THE GUN TRAFFICKER! HE HAD A BAGEL NAMED AFTER HIM AT A LOCAL COFFEE SHOP BECAUSE HE WAS SO FRIENDLY TO THE WAITSTAFF!

But enough about my great loves.

I want to tell you about two close encounters of a different kind. The kinds of dates you try to forget yet find yourself returning to over and over in the wee small hours of the morning. When you're alone with yourself.

It's 2001. I'm on spring break with some sorority sisters in Cancun. I was in the *only* sorority at NYU. A fact I hid from my acting friends for a year and a half. Everyone was very surprised when they finally found out because the whole point of going to a school like NYU is to get away from people who join sororities and fraternities. But I'm a joiner, and apparently I like to lie to dear friends. So we're at a club and I have been dancing with a towheaded guy—let's call him Steve—who seems to be the life of this

south-of-the-border party. We stumble back to my hotel
room and start making out. I tell him one sec and run out
on the balcony to yell to my sorority sisters and room-
mates who have passed out on lounge chairs poolside so
that they'll have choice spots tomorrow morning: "DEE
PHI EEEEEEEEE FOREVES!!"

I come back inside and find that Steve has jumped on
the bed and is lying on his back. Without much warning
at 'tall, he pulls his pants and underwear off. Mind you,
I'm still STANDING in my Billabong top and Aeropostale
skirt with my disposable camera still dangling from my
wrist.

He has a bit of trouble getting his khakis off over his
dirty Tevas; I help him, as he seems so determined.

Gentle reader, this man then presents me with a
mound of pubic hair so . . . tangled . . . so matted . . . and so
seemingly . . . disgruntled it takes my breath away. Beneath which is? It's hard to know for sure. I think it was
hard. But the swath of hair surrounding its environs is so
wild, so untamed, I have trouble getting at anything visually. There is a penis in there somewhere, but the over-
growth surrounding it obscures its largeness. Or lack of
largeness. All I can see is an angry mushroom cap. And
from where I stand, it's musky.

I can't help but giggle but successfully play it off as
though I'm being coy. I'm an optimist, a shape-shifter. I
need to get my head in the game. I come around to the
side of the bed and kneel on the floor, attempting to clear
the brush and get *at* it. To see if I can get his head in the

game. It's hard to excite something you can't see or feel, but, finally, a demented phoenix rises from a fur ball of ashes.

Now, I don't mean to body shame; surely I've had extra body hair here and there—haven't we all—but to keep such a messy basement and STILL have the audacity to display it with fanfare? His confidence, like that of all white men, is staggering. It's so deeply unfair to me that a man can hide his misgivings in clothing while women's bodies can't help but be on display. And while we are made to feel as though we should be ashamed of any imperfection, Steve doesn't seem embarrassed at all that *this* is the pot at the end of his rainbow. On the contrary! He seems proud.

Steve now begins thrusting his hips in the air, as if he's in yoga class about to bend back into a bridge. I realize this night is going to be . . . abstract.

His crotch heaves up and down repeatedly, as if we're having sex, but quick reminder: I'm not even on the bed. I'm no longer touching him, and he's no longer touching him. Seems no one needs to touch Steve for Steve to enjoy himself. And apparently, who he really doesn't need to touch is me. He's now grunting like an animal.

Maybe I imagine it, but I swear I hear the sounds of laughter from down below as my girlfriends chat and gossip about our night out. *They are still children,* I think. *They are still innocent.* And here, I have become a woman, being air-penetrated by a bearded potato wedge.

Steve is now lying prostrate and clawing forcefully at

the sides of the bed. Sensing he needs room, I take a step backward. He's gonna blow! Our eyes are locked in a horrifying stare. He writhes up and down and the bed thumps.

Finally, having reached his dénouement, Steve makes a sound I have never heard before. Nor again. It's not often you encounter a *new* sound. Most every noise is like, "Yeah, I've heard that." But not this one. This is a sound born of millions of years of rage and desperation. This is historic. This Is Us. I've tried many times to describe what I heard that night, but it really was more of a soundscape. It was Gremlin-esque mixed with a haunted howl mixed with the groans of exhaust from an old truck on its last legs? Nothing quite captures it.

Back at the scene of the crime: Steve's junglelike tufts of hair are now gleaming and sticky. And he looks at me, as if to say . . . "You're welcome."

FLASHING AHEAD, I am a little older and not much wiser. The year is 2003. The place is New York City. And the bed is IKEA.

I believe I am in love. I believe I've met the man of my dreams. He's tall and cute and a junior partner at a law firm, something that I thought was a made-up job they give people in movies. I think we are soul mates, because a few months earlier, while stoned, I'd sincerely proclaimed to June, "I just want to marry a businessman." And then just like that, he appeared to me, WEARING A SUIT at the Cedar Tavern on University Place.

This Bizness Man and I have been dating for four months. We're in my apartment, and even though I just said I was stoned a few months ago, smoking weed is not something I do often or even enjoy. I'm an alcohol person. (And a dog person. And I generally distrust weed people and cat people and find there's often a Venn diagram overlap here. Am I wrong???) But this Bizness Man has succeeded in getting me stoned off my gordos, and this time it is I who has stripped off all my clothes, while he is fully clothed. Yet I make no sexual overtures. Instead, I sit at my desk and stare at the wall and recount fond childhood memories. I think, *He's listening. He's really listening.*

And then he speaks. He announces that he'd like to keep things between us "casjjj."

"What does that mean?" I ask.

"Casual," he says. "I think we should keep this casual."

The rest is a blur, but I catch snippets. He needs to "get out there and be free" and "roam, like a cat." "I LOVE CATS!" I yell desperately. I grab my bra off the floor to try and cover up, but in my haze I only manage to hold it in front of my boobs. My lower half is still out and about.

"Free of *me?*" I hear myself say meekly. He assures me it won't be awkward if we run into each other out and about because we've got good "vibes." I affirm our vibes, but the tears streaming down my face belie my words.

For a second, I debate asking him to leave, but instead I sidle up next to him on the bed and say, "Hold me." I puppeteer his arms and force him to rock us back and forth, bemoaning what has been lost.

This is bullshit, I think. I went with him to Albany to visit his mom. ALBANY!!! I turn away from him and try to telegraph "You can't do this to me!" But he spoons me tighter and, I'll admit, I grind willingly back into him, inviting a last hurrah.

He accepts my advance, and suddenly we are making out with more passion than we ever have before, and it feels good; it feels right. Annnnnnnnd I am being turned over. I am on all fours. He enters me, and I nearly buckle from the force. I throw my arm out in an effort to keep from choking on my cloud-covered down comforter and end up having to bolster myself on the bed frame. It pops out of place. FUCKING IKEA!!!

I debate looking for the small S-shaped tool that came packaged with the bed, but much like my pride, I know I won't find it anywhere.

I return to the breakup sex at hand. It's exciting! I rationalize that this is where love and hate, fear and anger, fuse to become one! THIS IS LIVING IN MANHATTAN AND DATING A MAN OF BUSINESS!!!

It is at this very moment that my sweaty, "casjjj" gentleman caller whispers the following sweet nothing into my ear:

"Can I fuck you in the butt?"

"What's that?" I say, playing it off as though I haven't quite heard him.

He asks again in a clearer voice.

My mind wanders. I am on the beach collecting shells of pale pink. I'm playing school with my grandfather—

I the teacher, he the student—and with every correct answer, I give him one gold star. I think of my beloved Raggedy Ann doll, how she was missing one eye. How it must've felt to go through the world with only one eye. I feel closer to her now. I understand her now.

Let's recap. This guy has told me he wants to break up so he can roam the streets like a panther. Now he's asking if we can do something I've never done before. Asking politely, but still. I contemplate the question. It's a big ask, especially given the circumstances . . .

No, no, nope. Nopers. This will not stand. My mom fought beside Bella Abzug and thousands of unsung activists, devoting the better part of her *life* to getting the Equal Rights Amendment to pass. They failed, but I will not. I will stand the fuck up—for myself, and for others who lack my courage. For once, I want to be proud of the way I handled things. I want to make my mom proud. And my grandfather.

I turn to look at this titan of industry. I want to stare straight into his eyes and say this with conviction. In the darkness of the tiny bedroom, I speak. Nay, I roar.

"Yes," I say. "Yes, you may."

Cool Girl

There is no quantifiable reason why I think of myself as uncool. Except for that I clearly am. But I IDENTIFY in the bowels of my very soul as uncool. This is one of those, as Ms. Winfrey would say, "Things I Know for Sure" about myself. When I say the gap between myself and your Alexa Chungs feels cavernous, it's an understatement. Try as I might I can never keep up with the Rashida and January Joneses. How are they such? How does one become? Why not am I? Where should I attempt? What even is?! #Questions. The fact that I still use hashtags feels illustrative of my uncoolness.

An old boyfriend once told me that he hates when gorgeous celebs like Chris Hemsworth and Charlize Theron say they were nerds in high school, "when it's just like, really??? Guess we'll have to trust you on that one." My old boyfriend Paul had the diametrically opposite experience. "I look nerdy, so people always assume I was a huge dork in high school. But I was so fucking cool I was voted Prom King." I was only ever voted "Best Passer" by the coach of my middle school basketball team. Some people are just cool. Maybe they're born with it. Maybe it's Maybelline.

I try desperately to bridge this gap and make myself at least *appear* cool. Dress for the job you want! But coolness refuses to take, because it's simply not there for the taking. You have it or you don't. I once worked with a stylist on a quest to have a cool person put me in cool clothes. I thought I could hide in plain sight. She put me in chic high-waisted skirts paired with casual tucked-in tees and layered on lots of gold necklaces arranged just so. She even got me to purchase a head scarf, but whenever I wore it, people would look at me in confusion. As if thinking, *Huh. My eyes see and tell me those clothes are cool and yet the human wearing them screams the opposite.* Ms. Winfrey often quotes Maya Angelou, saying, "When someone shows you who they are, believe them."

After we broke up, Paul started dating a *very* cool girl, whom he is now married to. My God, is she cool. She has tattoos, she wrote a column for *Vice* magazine, she showruns an HBO show about female skateboarders . . . The first time I met her was at a party hosted by Sarah Silverman I felt very cool to have been invited to. His girlfriend was on the other end of the roof deck from me, but I was able to size up the fact that she was wearing a miniskirt in the dead of winter. Swoon. Two cool people had found each other. My ex was probably relieved his new girlfriend didn't insist on a musical rotation comprised only of the *Wicked* soundtrack and Billy Joel or sleep in long, old-timey, Kathy Ireland Collection floral nightgowns.

I know it's even uncool to say I'm not cool. Like, just accept it and keep it moving. Know your lot. Stay in your lane. I pride myself on being self-aware, so this need to move above my station feels particularly gross.

At an Emmy party (more cool things! Be impressed I was at one!!) I found myself sitting next to a cool girl. We got to chatting and she told me she wrote a sex column for a very chic online magazine. Check. She had platinum blonde hair. Check. She was aloof. Check check. The kind of girl who doesn't immediately chime in after you say something to provide commiseration or fill the silence. Cool girls tend to not lift a finger when it comes to social lubrication. It's as if because they're so comfortable with themselves they don't recognize the feeling of discomfort and therefore lack the natural instinct to put others at ease. A trait I deplore.

I looked around for a way out but this blonde and I were landlocked on an L-shaped sofa. Our husbands were in an animated discussion, so it became clear we would be riding out some more uncomfortable moments together.

I was surprised when she leaned in and confided that she suffers from major anxiety at social events. So much so that she would probably be sitting on this couch all night. I was free to go. Her admission made me so happy. Cool people have anxiety! I don't! I'm just a depressive! I win! She went on to say the reason for her anxiety was that "ninety-nine percent of people who talk make me feel embarrassed. Everything people say [noncool people, I read between the lines] makes me cringe."

Suddenly, I felt very self-conscious. I reviewed the last five minutes. Had I made her cringe with my manic retelling of the improbable fight my husband and I witnessed upon walking into the party between MARK BURNETT AND TOM ARNOLD? A physical fight!!! "How did I get so lucky???" I'd asked her. She had stared blankly throughout. I didn't understand how she hadn't leaped from her seat and run around the party announcing what I had just told her. The story was that good. And now, in hindsight, I felt stupid.

But outwardly, I nodded and said, "Yeah, I can see how it's hard to talk to civilians when you feel so embarrassed for humanity." My hands felt clammy. I started babbling, as I do when I think someone thinks I'm annoying or lame. It's a wonderful quality I hope never to shake.

"You wanna know the reason I'm not drinking?" I asked. (She hadn't displayed any interest in the topic.) "It's because I have to be up with my kids in the morning. And alcohol mixes badly with the medication I'm on for postpartum depression. I'm fine now! Ha! Mostly. I mean, sure, at an Emmy party, at thirty-nine, I can't help but think it may be time to find some radical acceptance around the fact that my dream of becoming Rachel McAdams or Kerry Washington may not come true." Silence. I continued to spiral. "Do you feel like you're walking around carrying the psychic pain of your mom and her mom with you wherever you go? The trauma of dead ghosts? I listened to this podcast that said the reason you can feel the pain of the women that came before you so acutely is because—get this!—when your grandma was five months pregnant with your mom, that's when your mom developed her own eggs. So TECHNICALLY—stay with me—you were THERE for most of your grandma's life and the entirety of your mom's! Your granddaughter could be in there!" I point to her stomach. More silence.

"Point being, I wasn't gonna drink tonight, but what's one glass? Or, actually, could I maybe take a sip of your . . . bourbon, I'm assuming"—cool girls always drink brown liquors, I find—"I think it'll shake a little of my own social awkwardness, which is clearly on full display! Ha again!"

She looked at me evenly. Cool girls aren't easily ruffled by unsolicited, off-the-wall personal revelations. Because they don't really care. And that's what's at the heart of my anger toward these mythical unicorns. It's as if they equate caring with weakness. And I do care. I care deeply if someone feels upset or embarrassed or left out. I not only care, I take on their emotions in what some would describe as a codependent form of trauma bonding. With friends and strangers alike! And this girl couldn't be bothered to throw me even a "Mmm hmm."

Finally, her husband came over and said there was someone he wanted her to meet/save her from me? Naturally, he was a TV Star. Premium cable. A cool guy. I'm sure he could smell my network stench.

And now I was alone. Across the room, David was really displaying his solidarity by having a big laugh with my old boss, Lorne Michaels. Normally, having no one to talk to would be my worst nightmare, but after my most recent encounter I simply sat, surprisingly unselfconscious. It must have been an odd sight. Someone sitting all alone on a huge couch as hundreds of famous people milled about.

But suddenly I was no longer alone. Suddenly, with zero warning, the comedian and actor Louie Anderson appeared like a freight train. "MAY I SIT DOWN???" I had never met him but knew him as the host of *Family Feud* and more recently from *Baskets*, Zach Galifianakis's genius show, on which he plays Zach's mother. He took a seat so close he was almost in my lap. He was in my lap.

Where was my husband? is a question I never once asked. I felt a calm, loving sweetness from Louie. He looked flustered but I could feel warmth had entered this space, where it had once been cold. I dug my tired H&M clutch (not sanctioned by my stylist) out from underneath us so we could sit more comfortably. He turned to me and said, so genuinely, "I'm such a fan. What was that show you were in—that very funny, cool show where you were so funny? *Happy Endings*? Who was that character? That character that was so funny and vulnerable?" he repeated. "Penny?"

I was taken aback. Lots of people at these parties say they're a fan and I say it to everyone I love because I think it's nice to express when someone has touched you with their performing, but I had never felt this level of sincerity. I told him how much I loved his portrayal of the mom on *Baskets*. "What I love, is that even though you are a man playing a woman, you aren't doing the slightest bit of a caricature. You *are* this woman. You inhabit the role so respectfully and deeply. You simply *are*. And it's such a moving performance." He smiled. "I'm playing my mom. She isn't with us and I always thought one day maybe I'd get to play my dad but here I am playing my mom. Well, actually, *she* is playing this part and I'm channeling her. One hundred percent." He was quiet and I saw he had tears in his eyes. It was such a wild moment.

Looking into my eyes, he asked, "Is your mom still with us??"

"No," I said.

"I'm so sorry."

And then he asked me something I realize no one ever asks.

"What was her name?"

"Kathy," I said.

He looked up at the sky and with a quiver in his voice, he said, "Love you, Kathy." And then he got up off the sofa and walked away.

What a cool guy.

A Saber Story

An old friend has returned.

That was the note I found hastily scrawled in my father's handwriting on a paper bag and taped to our front door. At age eight, I'd arrived home from school with a friend, and we were confused by this cryptic message.

An old friend has returned . . .

We walked into the house, expecting a visitor, but the house was empty. My mom was most likely shuttling my brother home from school. My parents had recently enrolled Fletcher in kindergarten at a magnet school for the "mathematically gifted," leaving me to languish in regular old public and walk home, because I was quote, "thriving socially." It's possibly worth noting Fletcher would later be kicked out of that school for eating some graham crackers that had been left out on a plate for the preschoolers, in an episode my mom called "Graham Cracker-gate." She would shake her head whenever anyone asked her about it and say, "It's utterly ridiculous.

Is being hungry a crime?" But before that family humiliation, Fletcher's mathematical gifts afforded me just enough time to wolf down an entire sleeve of Thin Mints before he and my mom got home, none the wiser.

With that out of the way, I called my dad at work.

What old friend? Who had returned?

"Look in the backyard!" he yelled excitedly through the phone. I yanked the cord with me to the window and looked outside. The backyard was also empty. The only thing that looked unusual was a limp piece of rope lying on the ground next to a tree it'd been tied around.

"No one's back there," I reported.

"Damnit!" my dad said. "Not again!"

He explained that by "old friend" he'd meant our beloved black Lab, Saber, and by "returned" he'd meant that Saber had finally come home, three years after having jumped the fence and run away. "It was friggin' eerie. I was on the porch, drinking my coffee, and he just walked up the steps like he'd never left. He still had his red bandanna on and everything! He looked a little older, sure, who doesn't, but it was definitely Saber. I tied him out back. Guess he jumped over the fence." (Pause.) "Again. Damnit!"

But that night, Saber came back to stay. My parents rejoiced at what was nothing short of a miracle. As dogs go, Saber had been pretty legendary in our household and even throughout our town of Alexandria, Virginia. He'd run away so often and caused so much trouble that my dad would put us to bed not with bedtime stories but with, as he coined them, "Saber Stories." His imagined tales of Saber's adventures "on the road" delighted me, but the real Saber Stories were just as astonishing.

Saber was never not trying to run away. In his youth, we also had a yellow Lab named Elsa, Saber's partner in crime. My parents both worked full-time out of the house, so neighbors were routinely snapped out of their daily activities by a flash of black or yellow racing down West Masonic View Avenue. "Grab a steak!" they would yell to a spouse as they took off after the dogs. Saber and Elsa were everyone's dogs, mostly because they had to be; Paul and Kathy Wilson weren't exactly *on top* of things when it came to canine care. Hillary was right. It takes a village.

One late August, when she was seven months pregnant with me and feeling miserable in the heat, my mom got a call from the front desk of the Holiday Inn off the interstate, asking if she owned two Labs. She said yes— were they there? She'd been so worried. (She hadn't noticed they were gone.) "Well, you'd better come down and get them, they're here," she was told. "No rush though, they're entertaining guests by the pool, jumping off the low dive."

This was a cuter inconvenience, but not every story ended as well. When my parents first moved from Kansas City to the suburbs of Washington, D.C., they were broke. With their brand-new puppies Saber and Elsa in tow, they crashed with my future godparents while they looked for a place to stay. One night, Mom and Dad and

Bob and Gretchen came home from dinner, laughing, until the lights came on and they stopped in their tracks, horrified at the crime scene before them. While they were gone, Saber and Elsa had DESTROYED Bob and Gretchen's apartment. Not just a pillow here or a shoe there, but its *entire* contents. Every blanket, rug, and treasure was trashed. What wasn't trashed was pissed on. Every square inch. Even the walls had been destroyed. The dogs had stood on their hind legs and scraped off the wallpaper in every room, from stem to stern. The dogs had torn up stacks and stacks of old *Washington Post*s that Bob had been saving for research, and the bits of newspaper intermingled with the wallpaper shreds, making it look like confetti covered the entire living room.

My parents were appalled. My dad found Bob's glasses, snapped in two, and pocketed them before Bob could notice. At the *very* least he could get his glasses fixed. The next morning they packed their M.G. Midget with every stitch of clothing Gretchen and Bob owned, dropped the dogs with my mom's uncle (a man my father would later tell me I wasn't allowed to be alone with), and drove furiously through the District, trying to salvage SOMETHING. To try and make SOMETHING right.

Before stopping at a dry cleaner, Mom and Dad parked the car in front of an optical shop and carried Bob's glasses in, as though they were rushing a small child into an ER. No matter the cost, they needed to be fixed immediately! They were repairable, and one small task down, they returned to the car . . . which had been broken into while they were in the optical shop. All of Bob's and Gretchen's clothes were gone. As well as Gretchen's cherished quilts, hand sewn by her grandma.

Sitting up with Bob and Gretchen that night "processing" over wine and Chinese food, there were tears, some yelling, and finally laughter as Bob emerged from the bedroom holding his glasses, a befuddled look on his face. "It's so weird," he said, "I broke these two weeks ago and they've somehow been fixed."

I couldn't believe Bob and Gretchen stayed in my parents' lives after this incident, much less became my godparents. "I mean they didn't *love* it . . ." My mom shrugged and then trailed off, as if to say "but what else could be done?"

What else could be done, really, but breed Elsa and Saber? "You just try to come over around Christmas and not buy a Lab puppy with a bright red bow around its neck—just try!" my dad warned. But even fatherhood refused to tie Saber down. Still, he ran.

Paul Wilson decided that the only thing left to do was build a higher fence. Instead of adding wood to match the look of the existing fence, my dad nailed huge rolls of gnarled barbed wire to the top and called it a day. A prison for his prisoner! This worked for a bit, but by the time I came along, a year later, Elsa had been given to friends who lived on the Chesapeake Bay, and Saber had learned how to dig *under* the fence.

As a small child, I had a complicated relationship with Sabie, as I called him. He slobbered all over my Tinkertoys, and it scared me how he'd bolt when the doorbell rang, no doubt to try and weasel out the front door.

But one day, Saber weaseled out and simply never came back. It was hard to believe that this time he was gone for good, but my family eventually accepted it and made their peace. "He's in a better place," my dad would say. "I hope he found what he was looking for," my mom would add, sincerely.

Until the afternoon three years later when he was found and lost again and found again.

My mom had a vet come to the house to check him out. "Yep, he looks about twelve, exactly the age Saber would be now!" His fur was gray around the muzzle, and that red bandanna was faded from a life on the road—a life of crime no doubt—but he was up to many of his old tricks.

"He still backs up in the kitchen the way he used to!" my mom said.

"He still loves to jump up on the waterbed and get in between us!" my dad cried. "It's uncanny!"

We were abuzz. Old neighbors flocked to marvel. An old friend-slash-foe had indeed returneth. *The Alexandria Gazette* caught wind of the story and ran a front-page photo of my parents with Saber on the front porch. In the image, Mom and Dad are smiling so wide, like Mary and Joseph in a nativity scene. I became a minicelebrity at school, where I casually told other kids in a practiced way that yeah, my dad was just on the porch one day having his coffee when Saber walked up to him after all these years.

"No one forgets where they came from," my mom told me one night.

"He went and did what he needed to do and then he came back. On his own timeline," my dad said.

"I KNEW he'd come back" was the phrase I heard them both say, almost arrogantly, to more than one person.

After about a month, the Saber craze had died down. Quite a bit more than I would have liked. As I was walking home from school with local bully Emily Ehrlicher, she took a break from shit-talking the other girls in our class to point at a flyer stapled to a telephone pole. "Hey. Isn't that Saber?"

LOST DOG the flyer read. BLACK LAB. LAST SEEN ON THIS STREET. My stomach sank. This wasn't good. I casually pulled down the sign, saying I was taking it to show my parents—definitely not so this person would never find out about *our* dog.

But at home, things had gotten worse. My mom was on the kitchen phone, her own sleeve of Thin Mints out on the counter, talking to Karen, our neighbor from one street over. Karen was telling Mom that a guy in a pickup truck had been driving around the area, calling out for his dog, and then asked her if she'd seen a black Lab with a faded red bandanna. Karen told my mom in her sweet southern lilt, "Kathy, you know I'm a Christian woman, but I looked that man in the eye and I said, 'No sir, I sure haven't.'" No one wanted to believe the jig could be up.

I gave my mom the flyer and we sat down at the table. Saber lay sleepily in the doorway. My mom said we couldn't lie—we had to call this guy, it was probably just a huge misunderstanding. Saber's new owner obviously didn't know we were his previous (albeit neglectful), rightful owners!

My mom called the number on the flyer and explained we had a black Lab named Saber here. Our Lab. The man told her the dog was actually *his* black Lab, named Moonshine. "Moonshine?" my mom repeated, and, if you believe nothing else, believe me when I tell you that Saber snapped to life and ran straight to her, practically leaping into her arms, in a way that said: "I am not Saber. I have never been Saber. I am Moonshine." In that moment, the myth came crashing down.

"How old is . . . Moonshine?" my mom asked. She listened then repeated a tough number. "Four . . . I see."

"Four . . ." my dad repeated that evening. Huh. So Saber was not only *not* Saber, but, in fact, closer to the age of a puppy than a dog in the twilight of his life looking to make amends to old friends. This dog was never Saber. Saber had never returned.

It was a lot to take in. All the magical thinking that Paul and Kathy Wilson generated could not make a Moonshine a Saber.

"I really thought it was him," I heard my parents muse aloud more than once in the months that followed. The vet who pronounced him an elder was embarrassed.

Everyone was bummed. Everyone except my grandpa
Red, who'd seen new Saber on one of his visits from Florida and told my parents they were "goddamn fools" if
they thought that was Saber. But as with any difficult
relationship that comes to an end, there are, in hindsight,
some red flags. We'd all gotten swept up in this enchanting Saber Story. And now it was over.

That summer we drove out to Culpepper, Virginia,
and bought a beagle. "It's time to get a dog," my mom
had said. "You guys are old enough." She acted as though
this idea had come out of nowhere. As though we hadn't
recently humiliated ourselves in the *Alexandria Gazette*.
Or as though a new dog could wash that humiliation away.

Josie the beagle turned out to be the type of dog that
actually wants to stay with its owners. David Sedaris
once wrote that if you happened upon his mother and
their childhood dog napping together in a deep embrace
on the couch midday, you might think you were wit-
nessing the aftermath of a suicide pact. My mom and Josie
were the very same. Josie wasn't going *annnnywhere*.
And if she did, whoever found her would surely notice the
ID number my mom had permanently *tattooed* on Josie's
belly. Not my mom's phone number—that could change,
she worried. But a string of twelve numbers that, if entered into a random veterinary database for lost dogs in
the state of Virginia, would lead you to my parents' information. My mom later said she regretted not including
her name on the tattoo, but Josie was a small dog. Until

she became startlingly obese in her old age. But that didn't slow her down. She lived to be fifteen. In fact, Josie outlived my mom, dying two years after her, on Mother's Day. Which I don't believe is an accident.

That's the only Josie Story we tell, and it's the truest and most magical one.

Send in
the Clowns

I discovered the franchise that would become the love of my life during the darkest period of my life. My mom had passed away a month earlier, and I was back in Los Angeles, the city I had moved to a day before she died, a city I now loathed. I had come back earlier than I wanted, from what was now only my dad's house, at the insistence of my on-again, off-again boyfriend, who was in charge of auditioning people for a new improv team at the theater I performed at. He strongly encouraged me to try out because he thought getting onto a team would lift my spirits. I'd have the opportunity to meet and pal around with other funny people and rehearsals to get me out of the house, and I'd get to perform. I told him I didn't know if I was up for being funny and/or being judged by my peers, but he assured me, "You'll get on the team in your sleep. Besides *I'm* the one picking everyone."

I did not get on the team.

So now, I was spending my days lying on a soiled couch in my apartment on Cahuenga Boulevard (cross street:

the mouth of the 101 freeway). Visitors and residents were warmly welcomed into the "lobby" by a sign stating THIS AREA CONTAINS CHEMICALS KNOWN TO THE STATE OF CALIFORNIA TO CAUSE CANCER, BIRTH DEFECTS, OR OTHER REPRODUCTIVE HARM. If I die, I reasoned, at least I'll be with my mom.

Across the street was an abandoned motel currently inhabited by a group of meth addicts. Someone had cut a human-size hole in the tall metal fence in front of it, and at all hours of the day and night, people from all walks of life would squeeze themselves through the hole and emerge sometime later looking like the living dead.

I lived with my dear pal from college, Laura, and though not on meth, we also resembled the living dead. Our place was a shitttttttthole. When we'd looked at the color wheel at Home Depot, the only color we could agree on for our common space was green. Within the green family the only shade we could agree on was bright stoplight green, which we used only halfheartedly to cover the walls, because no two lazier people have ever existed. To our surprise, while people hated it aesthetically several people rented it to shoot projects that required a green screen. It was hurtful to our eyes but helpful to our bottom line.

Laura would come and go, subletting her room and leaving me with a series of undesirables from Craigslist, one of them an editor of porn films. Editors are already the strangest bunch you ever did meet—they live in what I call "the middle plane"—but as I discovered, porn editors are even weirder. Mainly it was a pain when my TV shows were drowned out by the sound of two female performers repeating clichéd lines he'd try to get just right. I heard "Uh-oh, Tiff! I think we're lost!" one hundred times. But during this particular period after my mom died, Laura was home and could usually be found on the balcony, alone, with only a thirdhand, rain-soaked La-Z-Boy to keep her company. When she wasn't napping on it, she was sifting through a paint can filled with cigarette butts, looking for one with a little more get-up-and-go left in her, or as she called it, "scrounging for a partial."

Neither of us had much get-up-and-go in those days. Laura is a brilliant writer and the kindest person I know, but she is not without her quirks. She saw the original *Star Wars* part 1 and part 2 in the theaters each upward of twenty-seven times. She favored a diet composed solely of mozzarella sticks and Goldfish and was one pound and beautiful in the way people love to describe women in books and movies: "She didn't even KNOW she was beautiful!!" But Laura really didn't know, and there may not be a more charming trait. Our days of palling around together ended abruptly when Laura got a new job, running a big department at a new start-up called ShoeDazzle, which Kim Kardashian's tootsies were the face of. This dazzled us all, because it was the first decently paying job that any of our friends had. Laura was suddenly a woman getting up and going, with shoes to sell and people to manage. Every morning before leaving she would look at me lying on the couch and ask, "You think you'll be okay??" And I assured her yes, yes, just fine. But when she clicked off in her shoe dazzles and motorcycle jacket and the door closed behind her, I felt a crushing sense of loneliness.

Lying on the couch and watching garbage programming was how I spent my early days of mourning. By night, I'd be sleeping on a mattress I found on the street, a stone's throw from the meth den. I grabbed it because I couldn't bring myself to sleep in my normal bed, because nothing was normal. I dragged this soiled treasure up two flights of stairs and shoved it awkwardly into the closet, where it lay half in, half out. Something about sleeping in cave-like confines comforted me. Others would never dream of sleeping on a street mattress, but my brother had paved the way for this behavior. He *paid* for a neighbor's mattress after her husband had died on it. "Dead man's bed," he called it. Proudly.

Around my new (to me) mattress, I arranged all the sympathy cards I'd received, like a mandala of sorts, along with cards my mom had given me over the years, her many obits from papers around the country, and important knickknacks from my childhood. It was a shrine. I would lie awake praying for my nightly NyQuil to kick in. I took NyQuil every night. I never measured my dose, just took a swig from a sticky bottle I kept next to the bed and hoped for the best. (The bottle left many fluorescent blue triangle stains on the carpet, which would cost Laura and me our security deposit.) Sometimes I would page through my mom's day planner as I waited for sleep. She always kept a beautiful leather-bound agenda, nothing expensive or fancy, but I'd always loved looking at the pages and seeing her slanted handwriting, punctuated with lots of !!!!!s and a whole lot of plans. My mom was the kind of person who always had her choice of plans. She was in demand for plans. I now paged through the calendar like a detective, looking to see if somehow she knew she wasn't going to make it past September 1, reading about the future she would not have. The doctor's appointments she would not go to. The "walks with Carolyn" she would not be taking. "Fletcher's Graduation!!!!!!!" she would not be seeing.

I sometimes fell asleep holding it like a blankie.

Mornings (10:00 A.M.) would bring a burst of hopeful, manic energy. Maybe today would be the day!!!! The day I get back into life!! After seven cups of coffee, I would make huge plans for the day. "First I'm gonna do yoga, then finally shower, run all my errands, get to work on recycling the empty Best Buy boxes I've been using for trash cans, and return the 99¢ Only Stores metal shopping cart I found outside our apartment that I've been using as my laundry basket." Yes, today would be the day I leaped back into the world. And tonight would be the night I went to drinks with a couple of girlfriends, caught up on what was going on with THEM, and afterward diddy-bopped to meet up with some other pals for dinner. Maybe late-night drinks, too! I was back, baby!

By 11:00 A.M., I would be exhausted, lying on the couch, slat blinds drawn, soaking in the chemicals the only building I could afford to live in was serving up.

The only errand I actually completed in those first few months was one I reasoned was worth the effort because it would help lower future exertion levels. I visited my OB-GYN to ask for a prescription for something I'd read about online: pee pills. What are those? you ask. They're bright blue capsules designed to mask your body's urges to urinate, so you pee less frequently. Grief had me in such a state of lethargy I felt genuinely fed up with expending even the energy needed to go to the bathroom. How was anyone supposed to live like that?? Especially someone who had nothing else to do BUT urinate??!!

My doctor was a bit surprised by my request, but she could see I was in great need and in a full-blown emotional spiral. She told me they're usually only prescribed for the elderly and infirm—and in some cases, here in Los Angeles, to agents' assistants who aren't allowed to leave their desks during the day. I had no desk, but I had a couch, and I didn't want to leave it. After popping my pills, I'd gotten my pee breaks down to like three a day, and even though the pills turned my urine a fluorescent blue (not unlike my NyQuil), I felt this was an important, if small, victory.

Urination breaks eliminated, I was back on the couch and free as a bird. Now I could cry-watch *Oprah* without the whole rigmarole of having to get up, brush the Cheez-Its off my oversize Dolly Parton T-shirt, walk the two steps to the bathroom, and shimmy my big undies down to pee. They say after a loved one dies it's important not just to stay alive . . . but to THRIVE.

It was under these grim conditions, remote control in hand, that I came across two *lifelines*. One was a network called Bravo. The other was its new reality show, *The Real Housewives of Orange County*. It featured rich older gals who lived in a tiny hamlet I had never heard of (but now have engraved on an anklet charm) called Coto de Caza.

As fate would have it, I was one of the lucky ones who stumbled across the FIRST airing of the FIRST episode. And if I achieve nothing else, I'd like that fact included on my gravestone. (And I'd love to be buried with my pee pills, as it's really not gonna be convenient to go from there.)

On that first episode I met the women who'd become my lifelong frenemies, the first of whom was the "OG of the OC," Vicki "Whoop it Up" Gunvalson. A delightfully unhinged blond insurance agent who was burdened with an anger problem that eclipsed even mine. She intrigued me. Next, I was introduced to housewife Jeana Keough and her husband, Matt, a former middling Major League baseball player who we never saw because he lived in the attic and refused to communicate with his wife or family. He was like Maris from *Frasier*: never seen, but never spoken of kindly. Then came Lauri Peterson, a poor, dim blonde with a heart of gold who worked for Vicki, and later—in a triumphant twist Shonda Rhimes herself couldn't have come up with—married a man so rich she could buy and sell Vicki. Then there was Jo, a woman who redefined the word *thirsty*. And finally, a woman whose name no one remembers. I was hooked.

I watched the first episodes with my mouth open. Each woman personified an emptied-out purse. The detritus of their lives strewn about for all to see. I was shocked by what they were willing to put out there. But the craziest thing was that even though I HATED them, I also . . . LIKED them. Nay, rooted for them. And then immediately hated them and laughed at the destruction of their lives happening before my very eyes. And then rooted for them all over again. It was—and remains—one of the most rich and complex (and one-sided) relationships of my life. And they say you can't make new, old friends.

And then Bravo went and added another city! And another. And another. And new disasters of humans were revealed that put the other women to shame. They say there are no great parts for women over forty??? I BEG TO DIFFER. These women are Medea-esque in their emotional tenor and tiny in their emotional intelligence. Viola Davis should be so lucky to be given the opportunity to say to a party planner, when he challenges her idea of male models carrying her into the party on a throne, "Who gon' check me, boo?" Nicole Kidman would love to sink her teeth into these parting words after a fight with a gal pal: "Go home, wig. Goodbye, wig. GO AWAY. BYE, WIG." Glenn Close never summoned the rage Dorinda Medley gave us, after hosting the other housewives for a weekend in her Berkshires home that ended in ruin, when she threatened them with an empty vodka bottle, hands shaking, tears streaming down her face, slur/yelling at the top of her lungs, "I COOKED. I CLEANED. I MADE IT NICE!!!!"

Where else can you find programming *centered* around women, aged fifty-plus. And as far as fans go, the older the housewife the better. We are wary and often resentful when they introduce younger blood and try to get us on board with a gal in her late thirties or early forties. Those young upstarts can GET THE FUCK OUT, WITH THEIR ZERO EXPERIENCE OF THROWING A WINEGLASS IN SOMEONE'S FACE DURING A WINTER WHITE PARTY AND NO PRECEDENT OF PUSHING A FRIEND'S SEVENTY-FIVE-YEAR-OLD HUSBAND ONTO THE BAHA SHELF OF A BEVERLY HILLS POOL, ALMOST PARALYZING HIM FOR LIFE!! Nope. No room at the inn for anyone under forty-nine on this franchise, please and thank you.

Housewives casting is a delicate balance, though. I want 'em weathered, but I also don't want that wear and tear to show. I want them with skeletons in their closet, and that closet better have taken over two years to renovate and still not be "quite right." I want women who have lived a life, but to whom life has not been kind.

I took a musical theater class in college taught by a brilliant musical actress named Alix Korey. She asked us to bring in a song that spoke to us, which we would perform for her critique. I watched as classmates sang their thises and their thats. When it was my turn to go up, she asked what I'd brought. "'Send in the Clowns,'" I announced, proud to be performing such a "deep" song. "Sit down," she said. Shocked, and unsure if she was serious, I hesitated. "Sit down and come back in forty years," she continued. "You don't have the life experience to sing 'Send in the Clowns.'"

I took my seat, beet-red with embarrassment. But as I looked over the lyrics, I realized that I actually had no idea what they meant.

Losing my timing this late, in my career.
But where are the clowns, send in the clowns.

I see now the kind of woman who could sing that song. A delightfully charming, gorgeous postdivorce Sonja Morgan (once a *Morgan,* married to a descendant of J.P.) who now shuffles around in a crumbling, *Grey Gardens*–esque Upper East Side town house, more than once picking up loose TEETH that have popped out of her mouth. SHE could sing "Send in the Clowns." Actually, she could (and should) sing it in Countess Luann de Lesseps's endlessly revamped "cabaret show," while raising her dress over her head, as she is wont to do while slurring her poignant new catchphrase, "I don't have a chubby pussy."

No, this franchise has no place for a wide-eyed ingenue just off the bus with nothing but a tube of Chapstick and a dream. Housewives are just out of a repossessed Lamborghini with nothing but a tube top and a broken dream. And that's just how I like 'em.

But here's how I don't like 'em . . . I don't like any of my housewives to be pregnant, in therapy, or frankly, even in a yoga class. Too centering. At the drop of a hat I want them ready to drink so much they fall over a five-foot garden wall in platform heels and land spread-eagled in a large bush. I want them ready to HIDE in a bush and sob into the leaves about a rumor they misheard. And I want them to have full bushes. It's that simple.

The minute they have a come-to-Jesus moment—unless they're a bug-eyed Christian Evangelical named Alexis who Tamra Barney dubbed "Jesus Jugs"—GET OFF MY SHOW.

I also want my housewives to have run-ins with the law. And not minor ones. For instance, Teresa and "Juicy Joe" Giudice's legal woes and consecutive jail sentences carried the Jersey franchise on their back for years. Joe was ultimately deported and is now getting lap dances from broads in broad daylight, abroad. (My fingers are crossed for his new line of vibrators, which Teresa generously helps him peddle.) And that's just ONE storyline from ONE franchise.

Over time, the qualifications for cast membership have grown fuzzier and fuzzier. These days, not only do you not have to own a house, you don't even have to be a wife. ACTUAL ACTRESSES have joined the casts. It was recently rumored one such successful and beautiful actress was cheating on her husband (a man who claimed he could cure all cancer through radio frequencies IF the government would stop following him and just LET HIM

DO IT ALREADY!). The guy she was apparently cheating on him with, however, was not a guy at all but a former housewife! (She denies it. I do not.) And these are just the tawdry story lines. One *equally* riveting and important journey we fans have followed is the launch of, once again, our beloved Sonja Morgan's toaster oven product line, which sadly, as of this writing, has not gotten past the prototype phase.

Now, I beg you. Please don't tag any of these women on social media or tell them anything I've said about them (I MEAN YOU)! I want to talk about them behind their backs as the Bible tells us to. I'm scared of them! And happy I've never seen evidence of any of them reading a book.

I've spent hundreds of nights watching these women not change and not grow like a fucked-up *Truman Show*. My husband can't stand the sound of them screaming. "Really?" I say, *genuinely* shocked. "See, for me, their screams are like waves crashing upon the shore." I look forward to being lulled to sleep by the blaring siren of an ambulance pulling up to a house in the Bahamas to check on a woman who just stabbed her hand with a butter knife. I love drifting off to the sweet sounds of Kenya Moore or Ramona Singer ranting and raving. What exactly are they ranting and raving about? It doesn't matter. It just feels like home.

And that home is the house that Andy built.

Andy Cohen is one of the original executive producers and longtime impresario of the Real Housewives franchise. He is a modern-day Wizard of Oz. Our War-holian Godfather. Andy has been the puppet master since day one, without visibly pulling any strings. Which is where his brilliance lies. He knows he need only stand back and let these women live out loud. But he's also not afraid to step in—at precisely the right moment—to steer wayward housewives back into the fold. He is our fearless leader, a benevolent ruler who guides the franchise with cool, clear-eyed discernment, never afraid to cut even the strongest team member, lest anyone think the show hinges on them. Anyone can go at any time if they don't come correct or look alive. Anyone. See ya, Heather Dubrow. Get the fuck out, LeeAnne. On your way, Phaedra. As you were, Jill. And Dorinda, unfortunately . . . you didn't make it nice enough.

Andy's greatest strength, however, is that he knows exactly what's kitschy and funny about it all. Because above all, the shows are FUNNY. In an iconic moment during a Beverly Hills reunion episode, Kim Richards returned a plush stuffed bunny, still wrapped in plastic, that Lisa Rinna had given her daughter—because, I quote, Kim "didn't feel like the bunny was given with good intentions and therefore has bad energy." Andy watched with restrained glee as Lisa, in turn, delivered us a soap-opera-worthy SINGLE TEAR, complete with quivering lip, and then slow-walked off the set, saying she needed to "take a minute." Andy promptly gave that bunny a permanent home on the set of his talk show, *Watch What Happens Live*, where we can look at it anytime we want to remember BunnyGate. These are the moments we live for. And Andy gets that. And celebrates that.

He also understands that though we as an audience are here for wish fulfillment—a house with a pool in the foyer, the pageantry of Erika Jayne's outfit changes, Kyle's gorgeous husband—what makes the show work is the crumbling of that facade. When we watch them fight cheating husbands for alimony, rent houses they can't afford, Lori Loughlin–out their kids' college applications, and pose for mug shots taken long after the false eyelashes have come off, we feel utter schadenfreude. Their troubles are our delight. Which is horrible, in most other situations. But in this case, the women can walk away at any point (although we know they would rather cease to exist than quit). And so, while I feel bad if I lightly bump into someone in a coffee shop, and apologize profusely for having been in their way, I don't feel so bad laughing when women dressed in flapper costumes argue full-throatedly about who ate the icing bow off a birthday cake before it had been served.

I also try and learn from them. They're the Ghosts of Christmas Future. If we aren't careful, it could be us in Palm Beach on New Year's Eve—the anniversary of our ill-fated marriage—slipping out of handcuffs in a cop car after being arrested for trespassing. Because we were so drunk we thought the hotel room on the floor above was ours and cozied up in the bed and were discovered like Goldilocks. And when the police woke us up, we assaulted them and resisted arrest.

Their lives are cautionary tales. They've selflessly taught us what not to do.

But while we get to turn them off and go on our merry, it is Andy who, long after the cameras have stopped rolling, has to put up with what I can only imagine are the women's incessant texts and emotional spirals and jockeying for his affections and contract renegotiations and begging to be brought back. He was literally SHOVED by Teresa Giudice during a reunion, and yet there he was, not one year later, sitting across from her, conducting a meaningful one-on-one, Diane Sawyer–style. I tuned in for it like it was the moon landing. He is doing the Lord's work. I salute him.

And as Andy's legions of fans have welcomed his hand-selected muses into our lives, true friendships have been built around that fandom.

One of my closest friendships certainly has been.

While many of my close friends watched the franchise, I couldn't help but notice that one acquaintance spoke the language most fluently. Her name was Danielle Schneider. I knew her as an unbelievably sweet, hilarious, and brilliant improviser/writer/actress from the UCB. But one night over a glass of wine she revealed herself to be a Real Housewives . . . fanatic. From that night on we were no longer individual fans. We were fans *together*. I was in a romantic partnership with David and a Real Housewives partnership with Danielle. We texted endlessly during each episode in real time and called each other in between shows with the kind of musings and questions that had to be answered IMMEDIATELY: "Why didn't Kathy Hilton ever become a housewife? Could Andy maybe broker a sit-down between all three Richards sisters and attempt some healing?" We lived for talking about these women. But when our pal Paul Scheer suggested we do a limited podcast devoted to our obsession with the franchise, it struck us as a bit déclassé. Do a podcast about reality TV? We were arteests. But after giving it two minutes of hard thought we decided while we would probably just be screaming into the void, it would be fun to get some hot takes to the people. They deserved it. Danielle suggested we call it *Bitch Sesh,* and we set up mics in my breakfast nook and started talking.

At this time, I was struggling after the birth of my first son, who was now three months old. I felt like someone had taken a DustBuster to my hormones. All at once I felt more joy than I had ever felt in my entire life, alongside waves of crushing depression. This podcast devoted to utter nonsense ended up being such a lift for my spirits. I got to be creative without having to leave my house. Or put on real clothes. Once again, the Housewives gave me light during a dark time.

While *Bitch Sesh* began as a comedic project devoted to our psychotic passion, what happened from there is a testament to the power of the housewives and how great the need is to unpack and process its minutiae in staggering detail. People started telling us they loved the podcast, especially how seriously we take the show, BECAUSE, IF YOU HAVEN'T NOTICED, I DO FEEL IT

IS SERIOUS. From there, our reach expanded, starting when we were gifted a series of scathing emails among twenty or so moms whose kids went to an East Coast preschool, subject line: PAJAMA DAY. We changed the names and did a dramatic reading of the messages, and the insanity helped carve out room within the podcast for Housewives-adjacent topics. And then sometimes, things got darker and sadder. Danielle cried when she recounted the story of opening her yearbook and discovering a girl in her middle school had scratched out Danielle's face. I opened up about my postpartum depression and the guilt and sadness that comes along with it. The fans received this with open hearts and generosity and soon it became something . . . deeper.

A community was born around the podcast. The fans started connecting with one another and meeting up and forming online groups and splinter groups and splinter groups of those groups. They formed lasting friendships, some married one another, Danielle and I married some of them, some grieved with one another.

I think the main reason the podcast became so popular (aside from Danielle and me, OF COURSE) is because Real Housewives fans have a unique bonding point in that we all share a history. Granted it's a history we have only watched from the sidelines, but we speak the same language. We're like siblings who collectively get to witness our weird aunts and most offensive relatives behave badly again, with no stakes of our own. We get to feel a deep attachment to something we're equally detached from. And in that way, it's FUN. And between us there is instantly a point of deep connection. When I meet a fan, it takes us about two seconds to drop into what's really important: "Why *was* Lindsay Lohan's father in the background of the scene when Sheree pulled NeNe's wig off?????"

I hope I speak for all *Bitch Sesh* fans when I say, we're no longer Housewives apologists. We're tired of being judged for liking "lowbrow" entertainment. Michelle Obama is a fan of Atlanta and President Barack Obama follows Jen from New Jersey on Twitter. I will no longer feel shame over a pleasure I don't feel to be a guilty one! Life is hard. Together we allow each other to be the garbage persons we are and have always been. This is our nerd culture! Let Laura have her *Star Wars*! This is our Marvel! Our sports! The episodes are our playoffs, the reunion is our Super Bowl, and the off-season is a barren wasteland. When the NBA announced they had hatched a plan to quarantine players in Disney World to continue the season during the coronavirus pandemic, I said a quick prayer. Couldn't *our* players head to Puerto Vallarta and fight with each other under one roof like a Housewives All-Star Game?

What I will apologize for is forcing fans to watch Danielle and me sing and dance at our live tour shows. To pay for that privilege, in fact. The two of us share the same greatest unrealized dream: to be on Broadway. Since Broadway has said "no" to us, we make our fans say "yes." Despite that, the live shows are an absolute explosion of joy. Everyone comes in costume, dressed as various deep cuts from the Housewives canon, or in Danielle's words, "Andy Cohen cosplay." And at our last show at Town Hall in New York City, Andrew Cohen himself surprised us onstage. I lost my goddamned mind. The audience lost their goddamned minds. I have never felt a lift-off of energy like there was that night when he waltzed onstage in his cute lil red turtleneck. I dramatically fell to the ground but then I just lay there for a second. Taking it in. The connection. Danielle and I may not have made it to Broadway, but that night, you could have fooled me. Dreams do come true.

Even for housewives . . .

Though I may laugh at their foibles, I CRY when they win. When Mike Hill asked Cynthia to marry him. When Erika Jayne won the role of Roxie Hart in *Chicago* and cried with her former aged husband about how far she'd come. When Kenya conceived Brooklyn, the child she'd always longed for. When Scott finally proposed to Tinsley (even though he issued her a Sophie's Choice: marriage or the show). When Whitney brought her father to Mary M. Cosby's church and they both cried and cried. When Sonja finally got her fashion line into Century 21 (even though sadly on Instagram she is following Century 21 bank instead of the retailer and sadder still it closed in the wake of COVID). When Luann completed her probation and could at long last put the Tom chapter behind her. When Gia came down the stairs in her prom dress with a smile on her face, despite everything her family was going through. When Gregg beat cancer with NeNe by his side. When Shannon got over David's betrayal and started her own frozen foods line. When Marlo adopted her two nephews. When Porsha made the news marching for Black Lives Matter and getting arrested during a protest for Breonna Taylor. I can only imagine how proud that would have made her grandfather, civil rights leader Hosea Williams. She made us all proud.

And when I found out that Vicki, the original housewife I first watched from my couch on Cahuenga Boulevard, was being let go after fourteen seasons, I wept on the beach (two margaritas in). It was the end of an era. Even though Vicki is a truly despicable person, and did an Instagram Live from inside a club like a maskless wonder at the height of the pandemic, I can't help but have a soft spot for her. For all of them.

They have been entertaining me for fifteen years. And even though they don't know me, I have borne witness to the breadth of their lives. I've been there for them.

And make no mistake, they've been there for me, too.

Flyentology

I've always known better than to step a FOOT into a Scientology Centre or lay a HAND on an E-meter. Those metal cans won't be reading my past transgressions. Why? Because I KNOW that, were I even to turn into the parking lot, they'd have me for all of my present and future lives. I'd be "going up the bridge" in no time and attempting to convert family and friends, shunning anyone who spoke out against the Church, and throwing every cent I had at the giant human rights violation that is Scientology.

The reason I know better is because I am obsessed with cults. Everything about them intrigues and titillates me: the idiots who join them, the idiots who stay in them, the idiots who take their own lives in a mass sui— Suffice it to say, I love all of it.

The fact is, I myself live in the shadow of what I believe to be one of the world's darkest living, breathing cults: Scientology. Los Feliz, California, once the mecca of Old Hollywood glamour, is now ground zero for L. Ron Hubbard's failed screenwriting career. I can't throw a Clare Vivier clutch without it landing in the yard of one of the Church's towering, creepy, shuttered real estate investments. The Scientology Celebrity Centre (with an *re* because they are pretentious as well as unhinged) mansion, a huge gothic structure that reminds me of the house from Clue, towers over the improv comedy school I came up in, the Upright Citizens Brigade Theatre (also with an *re*—hmpf). You can't see inside because the windows are all covered by Gothic drapes. But whenever I'm at the theater or even driving by, I make it a point to glance up to the very tippy-top window, fully expecting to see Tom Cruise in silhouette and for thunder to clap. When I first started performing at UCB, I was strongly warned never to enter the SCC. Apparently, no one walks out without at *least* getting on a mailing list that—much like our alien souls, according to Scientology—lasts for eternity.

I realize I'm taking up the anti-Scientology cause a bit late in the game. Sure, I've always found it creepy, I was one of the first to buy a FREE KATIE tee, the only jokey T-shirt I've ever purchased. And when the book *Going Clear* came out and gripped the nation, I was disturbed, no question. But I have a *lovely* friend who's in the Church, so I sort of just turned a blind eye, the way one might have to pretend one of her (also lovely) family members didn't vote for Trump.

Life went on until one morning in 2018 when I was forced to confront exactly what's going on in that big blue fortress on Sunset Boulevard next to my son's preschool. What I learned horrified me.

My education began when I threw my brand-new

iPhone, overhand, into the sliding glass doors of my bedroom in anger. (The fact that Scientology is organized around the principle of impulse control is not lost on me.) The next morning, I had to get on a plane for my six-city *Bitch Sesh* summer tour, and as penance for breaking my phone beyond recognition, I would have to spend the trip, terrifyingly, phone-less. The only things I had time to do before my flight were attend my spin class at Flywheel and download seasons one and two of Leah Remini's docuseries *Scientology and the Aftermath*, which I had heard great things about.

Over the next seven days, as I traveled across the country, much like the "parishioners" who lived on Scientology's flagship base in Clearwater, Florida, and aren't allowed full access to the Internet or unmonitored contact with the outside world, I became a prisoner to my iPad and this show. A happy prisoner.

My travel companion was my dear friend and cohost of *Bitch Sesh*, Danielle Schneider. She wasn't sure what disturbed her more: that I'd broken my phone in a rage and had to use hers the entire trip, or the level to which I'd become obsessed—nay, possessed—by *Scientology and the Aftermath*. She'd look over during one of our flights to witness me sobbing as I watched a mother describe losing her son to the Church. Not only did this woman's son never speak to her again; he even went as far as posting videos on the Internet denouncing her as an SP (Suppressive Person, Scientology's term for any of its enemies). It was too much to bear, I told Danielle, thinking of losing my sons to an abusive church. (Small plea to SciTi: please don't take me down! Small plea to readers: if they do, TELL MY STORY!)

Danielle was also disturbed when I began asking our *Bitch Sesh* audience members, two thousand gals and gays who had paid good money to hear us talk about *The Real Housewives*, to chant "WHERE IS SHELLY? WHERE IS SHELLY?" (Shelly is the wife of Scientology's current leader, David Miscavige, and she has not been seen in public since 2007.)

I called friends (on Danielle's phone) and ranted and raved about my plans to take down the Church when I got back to LA, how they'd better GET OUT OF MY NEIGHBORHOOD!!!

Danielle suggested, correctly, that maybe I should . . . focus on our forthcoming shows and plot to take out Scientology when we got home. I nodded quietly and gave her phone back—but not for long; I needed it at 5:00 P.M. sharp LA time to sign up for my Flywheel classes for the week ahead, or else.

"Or else what?" Danielle asked.

"The best bikes go," I said, a bit too intensely. "I mean, I ride in the back row, but there are still better and worse bikes. And the best ones . . . go."

My immersion in *Scientology and the Aftermath* took me down some other roads.

I became bewitched, bothered, and bewildered by the enchanting Leah Remini. During our seven-hour car ride from Philly to Boston, I consumed her reality show *It's All Relative* and the audiobook of *Troublemaker,* her memoir, which had me cackling at Danielle, who was driving, "You gotta hear what Leah's up to now!" Somewhere around Quonset Point, Rhode Island, I began watching *The King of Queens* on YouTube.

"How can I get at Leah??" I asked Danielle, who rolled her eyes. "I need to express my feelings for her! Let her know I'm with her in this fight!"

I thought about any and all connections I might have to Ms. Remini. Through my agents?? Lawyer?? We once appeared together as contestants on a game show, *Match Game,* but I had yet to understand her cultural significance. My childhood crush, Scott Wolf from *Party of Five,* had also been there, so I'd had to prioritize.

Back in LA, I knew exactly who I could count on to help with this cause. My friend June Diane. I showed up at her door unannounced and said that we needed to talk.

I knew she thought something terrible had happened, or that I was coming to end our relationship; anytime I call her, she answers the phone with a panicked "Are you okay????!!!" So I reassured her, "Our friendship is strong, but I have to tell you something. And it concerns Scientology."

We sat down and I gravely explained my mission. At first, she looked just plain confused, because we were years away from the time when Scientology had gripped our nation. Also, she pointed out, hadn't Leah's docuseries been out for a couple of years?

"YEAH IT HAS, SO WHAT? WHO CARES? I'm mad about it *now*!!" June accepted this. "You come to something when you come to something."

Over a bottle of wine, I took June verbally through each and every episode of *Scientology and the Aftermath*. I cried, she cried . . . and at the end of my hour-plus soliloquy, she, UNLIKE DANIELLE, had the same fire in her belly. I knew she would. We'd been best friends and writing partners for over seventeen years, and now it seemed we would be partnering on a new, more ambitious project: taking down a religious cult.

"We need to start tweeting," June said, pacing.

"Yes!!!!"

At the same moment, logic caught up with both of us and our enthusiasm flagged.

"But if they . . ."

"Yeah. They're gonna come for us."

Life had knocked us both around a good bit and we considered ourselves tough cookies, but neither of us needed the thirty-seven websites the Church inevitably would create exposing every detail of our past.

"We'd be seen as Suppressive People, enemies of the state," June said.

Thinking it through, I said, "I do feel oddly comfortable with being an SP."

"Me, too," agreed June.

"I mean, it kind of fits me . . ." I said

"It's who you've always been," June agreed.

June got the ball rolling and tweeted,"WHERE IS SHELLY?!?"

It felt good. Emboldened, I tweeted, "Hey Tom Cruise, how are you? The organization you are King of is committing human rights violations, boo. YOU CAN'T HANDLE THE TRUTH!"

June made a face. "The ending's a little confusing . . ."

"From *A Few Good*—"

"Yeah, I know what it's from, it just didn't make a ton of—"

"Uh-oh."

Followers were already warning me to take down the tweet and friends were texting me.

"DELETE THIS!!!!"

"THEY DO. NOT. MESS!"

June held strong with her tweet. I immediately deleted mine.

She was disgusted. "What happened to strength in numbers??! People are being victimized!!!" (This type of thing happens a lot with me and June. One of us will become incensed about something and pull the other into our rage spiral. Then, sure enough, the later adopter begins carrying the mantle of hate even more fervently than the original hater.)

June was now DM'ing a woman she barely knew who was friends with Leah, to offer our support. Without looking up, she said, "Maybe it's hard for you to see the abuse and speak out because you're also in a cult."

I was silent for a moment.

"Do you mean—"

"Yeah, I'm talking about Flywheel," she finished.

Flywheel, for the uninitiated, is a spin class franchise. Three years ago, after the birth of my second son (with a cool seventy-plus pregnancy pounds to lose) I walked through their doors on a mission. To lose some lbs and prove to my OB-GYN, who'd labeled my pregnancy both "geriatric" and "obese," that I was merely geriatric. I'd only spun once before, and at SoulCycle, Flywheel's direct competitor. SoulCycle put me off. And this was before it was revealed one of its major financiers was a Trump supporter. Spinning in the dark while an exercise addict screams platitudes in your face was not my ideal fitness experience. Even though the room was pitch-black, my face burned with embarrassment. I was genuinely embarrassed that the other spinners around me would see me doing the exact same thing they were doing, that's how embarrassing it was.

But as June says, you come to things when you come to them! And when I came to Flywheel I was ready.

It was an instructor who hooked me. Amy Cooke or "Amy C." was my gateway drug. She was and is a PRESENCE. Her body is a sculpted work of lean-muscled art, and her personality is larger than life itself. I fell in love with her when I tried to check my cell phone discreetly in the middle of class. ON THE BEAT, Amy C. yelled, "Not today, bitch!!" and kept it movin'. She was a warrior, and for the first time I thought, *Maybe I could . . . be a spin person?*

I made an excuse to talk to her after class, apologized

for my transgression, and immediately fell under her spell. Her intensity was terrifying, but admirable; she somehow maintained eye contact even after I'd turned and walked away and driven home.

"Join my squad," she said. It wasn't a question. It wasn't even an invitation. It was a command . . . and one I was happy to execute. I felt chosen. I felt seen. I was smitten.

That weekend, I brought my friend Matt to her class. Matt was a committed SoulCycler, but I was sure Amy C. would worm her way into his heart. When the class ended, we hopped off the bikes and Matt pointed and yelled at me at an uncomfortable volume, "NO! NO. I DO NOT LIKE WHAT I'M SEEING HERE. You will not be leaving your husband and children for Amy C."

Had that thought entered my head? Yes, it had. Amy C. was gay, but more than that she was open for business, in a way that seemed to cross all sexual boundaries and states of mind. Her mission seemed to be to make everyone—man, woman, and child—fall in love with her, and then fall in love with their new body. Or vice versa—she would take it any which way. The crew of women in the class suddenly came into focus for me. All of these women were here for Amy C., too. Not really for the spin . . . For Amy C.

I told Matt he was insane. I would *not* be walking out on my life for a woman who barked "Clear Eyes! Full Hearts!" and expected us all to yell back, "Can't Lose!"

But the next thing I knew, I was at coffee with Amy C.,

detailing my fitness needs, of which there were many. She told me that not only could she help me, but in fact? If we teamed up, she envisioned a "Gwyneth/Tracy" level of success for us. "We could be Casey and Amy!" I laughed and laughed. Man, she was really something!

Pretty soon, I'd joined her exclusive boot camps and was contemplating a two-week, ten-thousand-dollar luxury trip to the Amalfi Coast to "sightsee and train with Coach Amy C." Whereas before I'd avoided eye contact with everyone at the studio, I was now the unofficial mayor of the place. The girls at the front desk would have my bike set up before I got there, and the owner would whip me playfully in the tush with a towel whenever I was late. (Quite the choice in the post-#MeToo world, but I let it go!) This culture for which I'd felt unfounded disdain had welcomed me with open arms!

I gave out high fives like they were in style. I complimented the young and the old ("Fun class today, Britt!" "Love riding behind you, Lois!"). I encouraged the bigger-boned ("Looking good, mama!"), and I was there for anyone who needed a friend ("Tell me your name again?").

There were some . . . requests that seemed to come with being on "the inside." I did a photo shoot with Amy C. that required me to re-create the iconic World War II "We Can Do It!" shot, only in ours I was kissing my "guns" and wearing a Flywheel sweatband.

My regular classes became like unmovable oaks on my schedule. I turned down an acting job because it would've meant giving up my 9:30 Wednesday. I was IN. In deep. But it was fun, and—more importantly, I told myself—it was healthy! I had a workout community, something I'd never dreamed of. A community in which shouts of "WHOOOOO" and "YOU GOT THIS, BABY GIRL!!!" leaped freely out of women's throats—mine in particular.

I felt alive. I felt like I was moving through life in a pink cloud. Everyone was so positive and supportive and motivating. And I'd only gained eight pounds since I started! Life was good.

And then the other spin shoe dropped. The *New York Post* published an article that rattled the Flywheel community. I woke up to several text messages from Wheelers and non-Wheelers alike, all asking, "HAVE YOU SEEN IT??"

The headline blared:

FLYWHEEL GROSSLY OVERREPORTS AMOUNT OF CALORIES BURNED IN A 45-MINUTE RIDE

My world came crashing down.

Class was a ghost town on Monday. Truly, only a quarter of the bikes were filled. The secret was out: no one was burning 600 to 700 calories a ride; it was more like 220. 220???!!!! I don't get out of bed for less than 300, mostly because I can burn that many just lying in bed.

The LA fitness community was turning its back on Flywheel. And when they turn? Ohhh sweet little baby Jesus do they turn. You do not want to cheat perpetually hungry gay men and women out of their calories. Pity the fool.

People fled. Amy C.'s once rousing pep talks from the pulpit now seemed more like desperate, frantic pleas to keep butts on bikes. Before, when she focused on me it felt like the sun shone only for me. Very much like . . . well . . . how I've heard it feels when Tom Cruise focuses his Top Guns on you. Now Amy C. seemed less like a messiah and more like a . . . fitness instructor?

One night during that dark time, I scrolled back through my texts with Amy C. She'd texted me one million times in the last year that she loved me and she believed in me and knew I could do this, that if I could just stop with the frozen M&M's and not let my cheat day be Wednesday Thursday Friday Saturday and Sunday, then I could do anything. Each message was accompanied by one million strong-arm emojis and the scrunched face with the heart on one side. We had had a good run.

But with clear eyes, I had to wonder: What was this??

I cut the cord. It was hard at first—I'd been spending a whole four hours a week with these people! But it was time to walk away.

Reentry into daily life was difficult. My friends didn't know what I was talking about when I'd say "All Day!" to encourage them during a hard time. It was Amy C.'s catchphrase. "All Day," as in "Never let up, keep going, all day." If they'd only followed Amy C.'s daily Insta stories, they'd know how meaningful it was!

But my friends felt like they had gotten me back. The

spell was broken. I struggled with survivor's guilt, but Matt counseled me, "You were a victim! Maybe the girls in the front row were burning two hundred and twenty calories but my guess is you were barely cresting a hundred." That was hard to hear. But I knew he was right. I'd bought over three thousand dollars' worth of classes, and when my reward points were finally high enough to cash out, all I got was a visor. I felt ashamed.

There was no reason I couldn't work out on my own, I told myself. I tried Training Mates, but it was too positive. I almost broke my back at Orangetheory, and the head of the old celebrity personal training gym I used to go to never responded to my texts. I tried the Couch to 5K app for three days and finally settled on a "Yoga for Healing Lower Back Pain" five-minute YouTube tutorial. It wasn't the same.

By the time I was fully deprogrammed from Flywheel, June and I had dropped the ball in our efforts to fight the war against Scientology. We had both turned our attention to other things. June was writing a how-to book called *Represent,* encouraging women to run for elected office, and I was seeing the sequel to *Mamma Mia!* twice in theaters. *Mamma Mia! Here We Go Again,* indeed! Also, truth be told, we were having second thoughts. Why make any rash moves that could possibly keep us from getting acting jobs? Hollywood hardly makes movies anymore, and yet Tommy C. still cranks them out. What if he suddenly had the need for a thirty-nine-year-old leading lady? Or a "friend adjacent to the leading lady." Out of an instinct for self-preservation, June and I decided to lie low.

And then. Heading home from work one day, I was stopped in traffic on Sunset when I laid mine eyes on another Scientology building, one I'd passed millions of times since I moved here but never really taken in. The sign out front read: PSYCHIATRY: AN INDUSTRY OF DEATH. The first thing that came to mind was: FUCK THESE PEOPLE. I felt so angry. So hurt. They preach the evils of any psychiatric help, be it therapy or medication, in order to keep their parishioners hooked on their fake version of therapy—auditing—which they record and then have at the ready to hold against anyone who should try to leave (as the gospel according to Leah tells us). It's all a circle of hell. And I'd been in a circle of my own hell two years earlier after the birth of my first son: postpartum depression. And after my second son was born, much like *Mamma Mia 2*—here we went again. Had I not taken medication, I truly don't know where I would be now. My mind flashed to Tom Cruise ranting like an uninformed lunatic on the *Today* show about Brooke Shields's use of medication to treat her postpartum depression. A deeply disturbing weigh-in from someone as unqualified to dispense medical advice as I am to spin in the front row. Medication saves people's lives.

But reflecting on it as I continued down Sunset Boulevard, I realized that it wasn't just the medication that rescued me. The medication got me off the bottom. But Amy C. and her sermons and her emoji-filled texts and the

camaraderie she offered women in a world where discon-
nection is the norm got me back into life. Flywheel was a
cult I could get behind.

I decided I would continue fighting. And spinning.
All Day.*

---

* **Note:** "All day" has been a little tougher to keep up these days,
since Flywheel has unfortunately shuttered its doors. Also I got a
Peloton. Which I have no excuse for not using. Still gobblin' those
meds all day on the reg, tho!

Hide Your Phones

"Men have anger." That's a phrase my dad used to say to me whenever he had an outburst over losing his keys or an altercation with a meter maid. Or after a driver would honk at him for going too slow and he would grind to a complete halt, blocking the driver from getting away; roll down the window; turn off his ignition; and dangle his keys out the window, as if to declare, "Well, now we won't be going *anywhere*."

"Men have anger."

To that, I now say, as an adult: SO. DO. WOMEN.

I'm furious. In today's climate we all should be. Have to be. If you AREN'T angry—amidst a global pandemic, systemic racism, and a disintegrating planet—there's something wrong with you, boo.

However. I have always been angry. Angrier than most.

Here are things I have done in crazed fits of fury, in no particular order:

Attempted to choke my college roommate in a Ny-Quil haze after I overheard her say she didn't think I was "fun."

Pulled two heavy brass sconces out of the wall by hanging my entire sixteen-year-old body weight from them after my parents told me I couldn't go to TGI Friday's.

Seriously contemplated driving my SUV through my home "for effect" after my husband suggested during a fight that I "calm down."

I may seem mild-mannered and sweet on the surface, but just underneath, I'm seething.

I didn't always label it as anger. My dad says as a child I was "challenging." "A handful," raved my grandfather. "Emotional," enthused my aunt Ann. I paid no attention to my mom's childrearing techniques from her dog-eared copy of *Raising Your Spirited Child*. I was too busy screaming at the fellow nine-year-olds in our neighborhood who hadn't learned their lines for my backyard production of *Cats: The Sequel* (rights pending).

My parents begged me to go easy on our neighbor Kristen. Her parents had recently gotten divorced, and her dad was living on a houseboat. Did I have to use the word *fired*? Couldn't I let her have a small role? "Fine!" I yelled. "She can play the telephone." Kristen would go on to dazzle a dozen citizens of Alexandria, Virginia, with how long she could remain crouched downstage right with her arm draped over her head as the human receiver and allow me to talk on her. I had—naturally—taken over the starring role she had vacated. Anger, I realized for the first time, could mean power.

It could also be exciting. I grew up in a spectacularly emotional household where joy and anger mingled seamlessly. My parents were successful, funny, and passionate people who taught me life should be lived out loud and all big feelings felt. No feelings left behind. My mom once tried to throw a dining-room chair at my dad's head, and I barely looked up from *Mr. Popper's Penguins*. My dad was arrested for screaming at a maître d' who wouldn't seat an elderly woman. Later, the woman told my father that while she was grateful he had stuck up for her, a stranger, the reason she was standing by the door was that she was waiting for someone. The upside to this was that as he was being dragged out of the restaurant in handcuffs, he had the presence of mind to yell to the patrons seated on the patio, "Appateaze me!" Meaning, throw their appetizers at him to see if he could catch them in his mouth.

I'm positive we all went to the movies after both incidents as if nothing had happened. A dark theater was a great postrage spiral landing spot for our family. Even if my mom was often asked to leave for laughing too loudly. Which also made her angry. "We're Italian," she would yell over her shoulder by way of explanation.

She called it "Italian"; my astrologer called it "Scorpio"; my husband called it "actress." All of these words to try and soften the blow of the truth. That I was an angry bird who would explode willy-nilly and often. As an actress, anger and "emotional flexibility," let's call it, had actually served me quite well. But I wasn't angry *because* I was an actress. (Although it certainly didn't help.)

The problem was I wasn't exactly sure what I was so angry about. It wasn't a constant state of being—in general I am quite optimistic and upbeat. Rather, anger felt like a tidal wave waiting in the wings, threatening everything in its path. I had no control over it. Did I *want* to yell "YOU ARE DRENCHED IN ENTITLEMENT!!!" to a woman wearing seven Cartier LOVE bracelets at a Beverly Hills salon who was rude to the valet and then chase her? Did I *want* to pen "newsletters" to my neighborhood shaming a male neighbor who wrote me a nasty note about my parking job? Why, yes I did! I thought I was a vigilante!

And it's not just strangers who would get the brunt of my thrice-yearly explosions. It was well-meaning boyfriends who wondered why we couldn't just "sleep on it and talk rationally in the morning?" Because I wanted to scream on it now! I still have deep regret over the few times I turned my acid tongue on my prized girlfriends. I think it was because I always felt like they could handle it (and they could, being patient and understanding), but they shouldn't have had to. My ability to maintain close connections with women from all chapters of my life is something I'm the proudest of. But nothing will threaten a friendship like screaming at a girlfriend "Your husband is a little bitch!" at a Buca di Beppo in Studio City.

Now. While I'm certainly not proud of that, we all know

anger simply isn't as palatable on a woman as it is on a man. And I'm angry about that. Angry at white men. Angry at all men. But I'm also angry at women who can't access their own anger and cover it by masquerading as little sweeties. And equally angry at women who display too much anger—rein it in, like I've had to! All versions of myself I have spent my life trying to wrangle and negotiate.

As I got older, even as I could acknowledge the entrenched sexism in the way the world treats an angry woman (and it's much more accepted from me as a white woman), I had to admit my outbursts were causing real problems. For starters, I lost a lot of phones. Whenever I'd feel a flash of white-hot rage overtake me, my first impulse was always the same. To throw my phone. My phone! My very lifeblood! My connection to all who might help me move through the very rage that caused the throw itself!

Over the years, I have thrown a Mountain Dew–branded pager out the window of my boyfriend's car on the highway en route to Rehoboth Beach. I've smashed my beloved bedazzled Sidekick into my dressing-room mirror at *SNL* and left a trail of BlackBerry crumbs in every shitty apartment complex in LA. I have only thrown my iPhone twice, once before my *Bitch Sesh* tour, and once in a tequila-infused rage in the Peninsula Hotel (but between us, on both occasions I knew I had upgrades coming).

In the beginning, these eruptions felt fantastic. Nay,

important. But over time the immediate release gave way to swift punishment. Each incident would lead to an emotional hangover that (much like my real hangovers) got worse with time. I got into therapy with the hopes of sobering up emotionally. Naturally she wanted to start with my mother. While I find it boring to blame everything on our moms (especially now that I *am* a mom), at the time, I was more than willing to open the hood and throw my mom under the bus to shift the blame.

We dove in. Was my mom angry? She was. But galvanized by it. After college my mom worked in the convention sales department for a Kansas City hotel; after a year she was the top salesperson there. But after spending several months training two male employees to do the same job, she discovered they were being paid $100 more a month than she was. As she told the *New York Times* in 1981, "I walked out. And joined the women's movement." As a progressive Republican, she became the youngest president of the National Women's Political Caucus: a bipartisan organization devoted to getting women into elected office and fighting for equal pay for women, a job she held for the first several years of my life. I'd traveled to over forty-seven states with her by the time I was three and was one time shuttled home from Phoenix by Sally Ride. (She wasn't flying that plane, just holding me as I screamed and cried from takeoff to touchdown.) As chair, my mom fought tirelessly to get the Equal Rights Amendment passed and became an outspoken critic of Ronald Reagan, calling him "a dangerous man." She showed up to the 1980 Republican National Convention, visibly pregnant with me and wearing a pro-choice button. (Suffice to say she would soon switch parties.) Ultimately, after eight years in the caucus, little movement on the ERA, and a political talk show pilot that was passed on in favor of *The Jenny Jones Show,* she left politics. She told me that being a full-time activist can be unbearably discouraging. It gets harder and harder to pick yourself up after pouring your entire heart and soul into change and not seeing it come to fruition. She got burned out. She felt defeated. And so, she walked away completely.

Although she changed course professionally, her sense of injustice raged on inside me. Though some of her dreams had not come true, she raised me to believe I could be anything I wanted to be. (Except a folk singer. That music made her feel nauseous.) This was a wonderfully liberating and privileged way to grow up. I had self-confidence for days. Self-confidence dysmorphia. Which is better than no self-confidence, but not every six-year-old feels comfortable correcting their principal for saying the word *snowman.* "Snow *person,*" I reminded her.

By the time I was in my early twenties I was a subway ad: if I saw something, I said something. It wasn't a good look, but no amount of hot yoga (the heat made me VERY. ANGRY), meditation (my mantra made me EVEN. ANGRIER), or candy (the crash INCENSED. ME) seemed to touch this particular issue. I couldn't get a handle on it.

But as I've gotten older, I can see now that anger was actually just the tip of the iceberg. It was often masking sadness. The sadness of publicly failing at my dream job. The sadness of cheating on a loving college boyfriend because I didn't know how to extricate myself. The sadness of my mom dying so young. The sadness of how far we haven't come.

And while I'm no less angry, knowing it's not the end of the story has made me less reactive. Anger demands you DO and sadness requires you be. For all my inherited comfort with anger, I find sitting in sadness to be excruciating. Anger is so much easier! It's a quick release and it feels good in the moment, but it can really hurt people, which also hurts me. But if I can manage to sit in the uncomfortable feelings that lie beneath, even for a millisecond, I am offered a tiny gift. The gift of a pause. And in that pause a crack of light comes in and I'm able to see things a little more clearly. I know to immediately turn my phone off or, if I'm driving, pull over and put it in the trunk both for its own safety and so I don't call anyone. And if I'm still mad after a few hours, great. I now know it's something worth being angry about. But the pause allowed me to gather myself and harness my anger so I can now aim it in an appropriate way. Sometimes even very powerful ways. I try now to use my anger for good.

Lying in bed at night with my son Max, we tell "Grandma Kathy Stories." He loves them, particularly the ones about the times my mom flew off the handle. Like when she shamed a woman at a baseball game who told her she was cheering too loudly. "NO ONE LIKES A HALL MONITOR!" But last night when he asked, I felt the familiar rush of anger. How could I communicate the loss of someone he had never met? How unfair it was that he'll never get to feel the force of her love. And how she'll never get to see his beautiful sweet face, frozen in a half smile, as though you and he are in on a joke no one's even told yet. I didn't grab my phone. I started to cry. I wanted to say something to him, to tell him why I was crying or that it was okay to be sad, but instead we just sat there in silence.

Finally, he said, "Hey Mama, tomorrow can we build that car I imagined? The one that has a hot tub and can go to space and has a snack bar?" It was the kind of jarring subject change kids have no problem making. I once acted in a play a nine-year-old wrote and had to say the line "Grandpa has cancer. What's your favorite kind of ice cream?" "Yeah," I answered Max, wiping my eyes. "We sure can."

"But don't worry," he said, "I'm going to paint lots of pictures of Grandma Kathy and hang them all over the car for you."

I thought of my mom's legacy. Of my own. And how, hopefully, as generations pass, the way in which we process trauma transmutes and the defeat of the grandmother becomes the anger of the mother becomes the sadness of the son. And so on.

Maybe that's progress.

Expect a
Miracle

"You have to get rid of all your drinking glasses. And your coffee mugs and your S'well bottles. They must all be replaced with mason jars."

I nodded and listened intently as a woman rifled through my kitchen drawers, organizing them. Well, not organizing, per se, but rather, as she put it, "whispering" to my cabinets. In order to transform the energy of my kitchen, obviously.

After the birth of my first son, I decided that I needed to learn how to cook. I was hoping to learn how to make a few healthy-ish meals for our family or at the very least defrost a fish stick. My Italian grandma was an incredible chef. My mom made tacos so many times that when I asked my middle school friend Meg if she wanted to come over for dinner she asked, "Is your mom making tacos . . . again?" Every night in our house was taco night. But who am I to scoff. I CAN'T EVEN MAKE TACOS! Which is why I had paid a woman who called herself "The Scullery Whisperer," upwards of two thousand dollars to help me. She came highly recommended by a friend who told me, rather cryptically, "She'll teach you how to cook and so much more." I wasn't sure what the "so much more" meant but I did know I was a lazy piece of shit who apparently couldn't open the Internet or a book and look up a recipe like the rest of the world. And so, here we were. The Scullery Whisperer was a fifty-something willowy brunette with a rebellious streak of purple in her hair the way white women like to do to "be crazy!"

"What the hell is this??? Is this a *metal* spatula??" The S.W. shuddered and threw it on the floor. She surveyed a crowded cabinet and pulled out a large glass pitcher with a dispenser I had received for my wedding (the only wedding gift I'd been allowed, as my husband insisted on charitable donations instead of gifts . . . eye-roll emoji). With her eyes closed and the pitcher in her hands, she felt out its place in my kitchen.

She opened her eyes and declared, "This will be the focal point of your hydration station."

If you're wondering how I got here, you're not alone. I'm wondering, too! When I first moved to Los Angeles I had merely dabbled in the spiritual realm, if at all. But as luck would have it, early on I was introduced to a woman who would become a lifelong friend and my emotional lifeline, the fantastic "heart-centered" astrologer Heidi Rose Robbins. As healers go, Heidi is *the* most lovely, talented, and grounded of them all—with two well-adjusted kids and a hot husband to boot. She has predicted things large and small for so many people in my life. Based entirely on the stars, she determined a friend struggling with infertility would in fact conceive (she did). She broke the news to a girlfriend of mine that she was headed into a "two-year descent" (she was), and told me during our first session that my Virgo in the sixth house craved order and beauty, and if I would just clean out my car once a week (ridding it of forks, blazers, bras, leftover rotisserie chickens, and banana peels), I would feel a lot better. I followed her advice, and the tide immediately turned in terms of how I felt about myself. I'd been a proud, easy-breezy slob, who celebrated not giving a ferk. But with the car garbage gone, my life slowly started changing. This is not hyperbole. Order ushered forth the ambitious type A control freak I'd always been, the true self I'd been masking out of laziness. Deep!

I should have stopped at Heidi. But she was my gateway drug and I was now a full-fledged seeker. My mind and spirit were open for business. I suddenly believed in anyone and everything. My obsessive self-help phase coincided with the period after my mom died. Those dark, lonely years found me suddenly with a real income but zero stability. My erratic high/low confidence wasn't serving me in either direction and I felt a general sense of unrest. Unease. And at night, I felt a cavernous emptiness. So if the darkness could be staved off and the demons kept at bay with a class, product, or consultation, I enrolled with Tracy Flick–like diligence. I have journals upon journals upon journals of notes taken during healing sessions of all stripe that prove . . . only how bad my handwriting is.

I threw my money at an astonishing series of wackos across this disgusting, concrete strip-mall parking lot known as Los Angeles and I was devoted to every single one of them. My husband says I am "a magnet for the unwell." (Something I oddly take as a compliment.) And luckily these new gurus were not in short supply. Of course they weren't—the city of angels also happens to be the city of broken dreams (mine included). In the 1800s, people migrated west for the promise of hope and gold, and not much has changed since then. I believe (??) it was k.d. lang who said in a song or interview (I'll admit my sourcing could be verified by no one at HarperCollins) that people come to California either because they have dreams of making it big or because their dreams have shattered and they're running from the pieces. And California is about as far as you can go. It's right on the edge. And so are the people.

I fell prey to them ALLLLL, sometimes dippin' a toe, but mostly diving right on in.

There were the S Factor classes, which turned out to be just pole dancing lessons for the wildly uncoordinated.

There was the Alexander Technique, where strangers wiped down my entire body with their palms, including the groin area, using broad strokes and then "released my head." (A chiropractor later asked me why the vertebrae in my neck were stretched like frayed wires, then said simply, "This can't be fixed.")

I attended group therapy with June, once a week for a YEAR. As a group we were taught the Grinberg Method, a methodology that trains your body to recognize its physical responses to stress, anxiety, anger, and depression, thus lessening the intensity of these emotions. That all sounds well and good (and it werks by the by), but in practice, you watch someone sit in a chair and "go into their pain." Meaning they accentuate a shoulder, let's say, and then go FULL TILT into the feeling of abandonment they felt as a child. They scrunch and contort their faces into what looks like a painful orgasm, often drooling and writhing, while the rest of the class sits on yoga mats nodding and "mmmmm'ing" at breakthroughs.

There were at least a hundred (prepresidential campaign) Marianne Williamson seminars, where I picked up my life's mantra. As I walked into her weekly lecture one night, bewildered and distraught from who the hell knows what, a random woman was lingering in the doorway. As I approached, the woman touched my arm, leaned in, and whispered in my ear, "Expect a miracle." I was taken aback but promptly made bumper stickers featuring the phrase for all my friends, I loved it so much. Don't hope for a miracle—EXPECT one.

It was like I was *trying* to throw my money away. There were tarot card readers, shamen and shawomen, Reiki healers, empaths, and nonaccredited spiritualists of all kinds. One psychic told me to break up with my boyfriend because we'd been twins in a past life, but neglected to tell me that during our session my car had been towed.

And then there were the retreats. Oh, how there were retreats. Wellness retreats, fitness retreats, yoga retreats, spiritual journeys, Miraval (on the advice of Oprah), an Outward Bound knockoff, and of course Heidi's astrological retreats . . .

Before I continue, I'd like to take a moment to address those of you who might be noting the disturbing, astounding, and likely alienating amount of white and class privilege these experiences represent. I couldn't agree with you more, and I'm laying all this out in an effort to be truthful and for a laugh. At my expense, as always!

So. In 2012, my Scorpio sun and I traveled to Ojai, California, for an all-women astrological retreat that my girlfriends June and Kulap had been on the year before and raved about. When our group met in "circle" the first night, Heidi explained that she had given us new names, and we weren't to call each other by our real ones. I became Rosebud. My friend Katya was now Kashmere (spelled with a *K*—perhaps inspired by the Kardashians, I told her).

Over the course of the weekend we did all the usual things you do on a retreat with twenty strangers ranging in age from nineteen to eighty-six. We were paired off and instructed to dance sensually with our partner, eyes closed, to draw out each other's sexuality. I'm not a big toucher in general. In high school, my girlfriends were always trying to hold hands with me. Ugh. They dubbed me Limp Hand. But here, I had no choice. I repeated what a cognitive behavioral therapist once told me to repeat in difficult situations: "This is the moment I find myself in."

I was partnered with a vibrant elderly woman nicknamed Sweet Home Alabama and felt like I was in drama school again, although I don't think even Stella Adler would've asked this of us. I found my way into our dance, though, and began to trace the curve of Sweet Home Alabama's back delicately. I moved lower and began to knead her legs through her slacks, attempting not to brush too close to her nethers. It was tough. But not as tough as what would come next, when we all had to rock and sway a grown woman nicknamed "Let It Be" in a blanket while she scream-cried as we sang "Amazing Grace" to draw out her Capricorn.

All jokes aside, it was a *fantastic*, life-altering retreat. By the end, I felt so close to each of the women. This always happens. I pride myself on being a seeker, "but not, like, crazy." At the start of any new group venture I prefer to play the part of "field reporter" and keep my distance until I can get a read on how many kooks are present. But by the end, I'm crying during their breakthroughs and rocking women in blankets of my own volition. In the mix. I become the mix, actually. The kookiest of kooks.

During the goodbye circle the last morning of the retreat, we all went around and shared what had resonated most with us. I offered that I appreciated the beautiful way Heidi helped me find some compassion for myself through the stars. And how she had urged me to be more discerning. She said while it's wonderful I'm so open and take on everyone and everything, she wanted me to view new friendships and opportunities "in the cool clear light of day." It's stuck with me since. Not everyone or everything has to be a yes. What a relief. The other women smiled at me. And I smiled back. It was such a warm atmosphere of support and love. Each woman had grown in ways large and small, and there was a peaceful, almost meditative air to the room. We'd all brought our coffees to the circle, which felt cozy. I looked around at The Greatest Depths Possible and Walking On Broken Glass and smiled. But someone was missing . . . Who was it . . . ? Violet Vibes was there . . . and there was No Way Through But Through. But where was Red Serpent??

Red Serpent and I had come the furthest together, having first circled each other as two angry, jealous Scorpios tend to do. But while I had a Taurus moon to ground me and a Capricorn sun to steady me, Red Serpent was a triple Scorpio. I wouldn't wish that on my worst enemy. I loathed her rageful, erratic energy. She challenged Heidi at every turn and drenched us in her toxicity.

Red Serpent would routinely not be able to leave an exercise or moment behind, and so when we would all transition to the next thing, she would have to walk outside the glass doors to pace, weeping and cursing, for quite a while. It was . . . uncomfortable. She looked nuts, too, and I felt that in this instance, I could most definitely judge a book by its cover. But over the weekend, as is my frequent pattern both because of my lack of boundaries and because I can be way too judgmental, I'd not only taken Red Serpent under my wing, but also embraced her. I liked her "spunk." It was I who led the standing ovation during her performance in the emotional talent show on the last night. She wore a floor-length rabbit-skin coat and opened her piece with a bang by brandishing a sword. I had no idea where she'd gotten those items, as all I'd packed was a pair of lululemon pants and my oversize Adele T-shirt. Which was actually useful, because for my piece I decided to sing Adele's version of "Make You Feel My Love" while holding a picture of my fiancé and crying. Let she who is without sin cast the first stone.

But now Red Serpent was missing from the circle. It felt weird, not being eaten alive emotionally by the darkest presence I'd ever encountered. Still, we moved on to our last exercise, cracking open papier-mâché eggs, chosen for us at random, to reveal the simple message inside. Mine was "Blazing Forgiveness."

Just as my egg split open, the door flung open violently. Red Serpent stood before us, on FIRE. She was holding an empty coffee cup, and she was seething. Even Heidi, who can hold a space like no other, was alarmed.

"Who took it???" Red Serpent growled.

"Who took what?" Heidi asked her.

"WHO TOOK THE LAST CUP OF COFFEE!!!????"

Silence.

It was a big enough group it would be hard to know who had taken it. (Probably me, in hindsight.) "ANSWER ME!!! WHO LEFT ME WITH NOTHING???" I remembered that Red Serpent had said the first night that being left out triggered her abandonment issues. It was hard to understand how someone taking the last cup of coffee could be seen as an alienating act, but as someone who needs caffeine the second me eyes peek open, I could get there. She stormed from the room, and we heard a car door slam and brakes squeal as she peeled out of the driveway. Toward Starbucks, maybe? Or was she leaving altogether???

Heidi paused and then said that all the Scorpios in the room could learn from this. She explained gently, "It's very Scorpionic to ruin good things at the last second." This rang true; I barely ever concluded a nice weekend trip with family or friends without burning it all down in the last two minutes. Was this what I looked like??

When we heard a car return twenty minutes later, we all stopped talking, barely breathing. There was a ruckus in the kitchen and then Red Serpent flung the door open again, almost tearing it from the hinges. She was carrying a (very large) coffeemaker under one arm in a football hold, the cord dragging behind her. In her other hand was a bag of coffee. She slammed the coffeemaker down on the ground next to an open outlet and jammed the cord in, angrily pressing the different buttons to get it brewing. "I think it needs water," one of us said. "I'll grab a filter," someone else offered. We all waited until we heard the familiar rumblings of the machine starting up. It gurgled, and finally, the first drop hit the cup. And with that, Red Serpent finally laid down her metaphorical sword and began sobbing. No one moved to wrap her in a blanket and rock her.

Two days later, Heidi sent out a group email asking how everyone had "landed emotionally from the weekend." Everyone wrote back what fun they'd had and how much they'd grown. Red Serpent was the last to respond and when she did . . . it was in the style of Beat poetry:

BLACK.

black as the blackest dark roast,
the all-too-familiar Spiraling Darkness.
it drank me deeply.
    home.
cream added to coffee. black yielding to light brown.
collapse.
a bracingly chilly walk to a
vista. the long view. 360-degree clariTEA. processing,
      witnessing, tears, revelations.
Grind the beans. Drink the cup and be filled.

Powerful stuff. No one responded. Which brings me back to my first session with The Scullery Whisperer. Scullery Whispering, she told me, is all about the healing that can happen through the excavating of one's food story as it relates to their mother. "We all carry the psychic burdens of our ancestors. We carry them in our bodies and they show up in the way we tend to our own hearth and feed ourselves and our families."

"Hmm. Could you maybe teach me how to grill chicken?" I asked, hopefully.

Over the course of three full days, we reorganized and reenergized my kitchen, a process my four-month-old wailed through from his seat in one of those dangerous slanted springy baby seats on the kitchen table. Bags of basic and utilitarian metal kitchen tools were donated and replaced with wooden versions for better energy, and my metal countertops were draped with scarves so my eyes didn't fall upon the harsh surface and contaminate my vibes. She told me she only wished she had known me when we were renovating because she would have advised I rip out the metal altogether. Could I think about it? The windowsill was given a "spatial lift" with beeswax candles and many, *many* expensive items ordered from Williams-Sonoma.

"Any idea how to make oatmeal?" I asked as we transferred chickpea fusilli into glass canisters.

"Our bodies tell stories," she responded. "What was your grandmother's food story?"

I thought about it. My grandmother was a bit agoraphobic and a fabulous cook, so she spent most of her days in the kitchen, making delicious Italian food from scratch. Feeding people was her love language. She had more time than me, I rationalized, since . . . she never left the house.

"And what was your mother's food story?"

That one was less clear. Her version of second-wave feminism dictated that she swing the pendulum as far as possible from her domestic stay-at-home mother. She fed us, of course, and took wonderful care of us, but her disdain for cooking often led to very unhealthful eating. Who amongst?

"And what's *your* story?" the S.W. asked.

My story was caught somewhere in between my mother's and my grandmother's. The words *Crock-Pot* and *meal prep* made me shudder, but the reality was I had a child now and that resistance could only end up hurting my baby son. I wanted to at least *attempt* to feed him healthy foods. I knew my limitations. I would not be making baby food from scratch. Moms who do this trigger me in the same way celebrity moms who post AGGRESSIVE photos of the perfect lunches they send their kids off to school with do. Lunches only someone with too much time and too many resources could be capable of. My therapist said *I* should spend some time thinking about why I feel these posts are aimed at me. But I probably won't. Because THEY KNOW WHAT THEY'RE DOING.

The Scullery Whisperer interrupted my homicidal thoughts.

"It's okay to shed your mother's narrative. And create an entirely new one."

This hit me. But also seemed like a lot of work? "Give yourself the permission to straddle the masculine and the feminine worlds," she continued. "When you step through the threshold of your home, allow yourself to inhabit the feminine. Because we are all so very hungry but it's not for food." I nodded. What she was saying genuinely resonated, but I couldn't get past the fundamental, more shallow reason I had hired her.

"But . . . how do I *cook*??" I asked her. "Where do I start? I can barely—"

She cut me off. "Stop spending time feeling guilty that you don't fucking cook and just COOK!"

I thought about that. I would often boil herbs and cinnamon on the stove to make the house smell homey, like someone had been cooking. This was almost as much work as actually cooking. It reminded me of high school, when it had occurred to me that it took more effort to snake headphones through the sleeves of my puffy winter coat so I could hear myself SLOWLY reciting a poem I had prerecorded, so I could appear to have memorized it for my English exam. It might be easier to just learn the poem.

While I wasn't getting many practical cooking tips from The Scullery Whisperer, I was getting *something* out of these sessions. When we did cook, she would bat the pen out of my hands if I tried to take down recipe directions because they "lived up here and in here," gesturing wildly from her head to her heart.

After our sessions were up, she announced that she would need two to three more workshops with me, this time at her home in Culver City (an hour's drive). Under her spell, I accepted immediately. In Culver City, she would start each session by making me walk around her backyard barefoot, "really seeing the trees," then have me lie down in Savasana on the cold, hard floor of her sunroom, "settling" while she made us tea. One time she had me sit on a packing crate in her dank cluttered garage and paint "from my inner child." I clearly embraced the assignment with gusto, as my husband later mistakenly put the piece in a box labeled KIDS ART.

After wrapping up the arts and crafts day, I was sitting in my car on her tree-lined street, "in silence with myself," upon her recommendation, when my phone dinged with a Venmo request. It was The Scullery Whisperer requesting $1,400.00. I sighed. Once again, I found myself in something resembling a cult. Thankfully no one branded my crotch, but no one taught me to cook either. I knew I had no one to blame but myself. This had all been my choice. Because I was capable of making choices. And I had been making some bad ones. Heading home in rush-hour traffic, late for dinner with my son, I heard a voice. A small voice at first, so small I barely knew where it was coming from, but it was telling me something. It was my voice. And it was telling me just because someone says they know something doesn't mean they do. Or that it's right for me. And this incessant searching had brought me further afield from my North Star—which was what I was paying people handsomely supposedly to help me find. Services rendered: nonsense. What if I didn't need intuitives or horse therapists to tell me what to do?

In that moment, I knew I had sought long enough. In all the wrong places. And what was it I was even searching for, exactly? I swore off healers completely.

For a couple of weeks.

HOW COULD I *not* take a friend up on her suggestion to drink ancient cactus runoff called San Pedro (described as "Ayahuasca lite") in a dirty backyard in Van Nuys with her and thirteen strangers? I HAD TO! These were once-in-this-lifetime opportunities. The young hippie woman leading the ritual explained that "San Pedro is 'the grandfather energy.' On it, you will receive messages from the universe. You can ask specific questions or simply let the messages appear."

We all took turns drinking the sacred juice from Peru and dry heaving in the bushes. It wouldn't be long before I was hallucinating through a hell spiral of my past and former lives! I looked over at our leader, who had promised to "guide us through ourselves." I couldn't help but notice she had stripped down to a bikini, something I'd never seen a healer do. It made more sense when she announced she had decided last minute to "partake." Soon she was weeping and snotting into a pile of leaves, effectively cutting the cord between us and the reality we had all just left behind. There was no one to take care of us. No one to look to. My worst fear had come true. *I am all alone,* I thought.

Ask me for a message, I suddenly heard myself say to myself. It was me, but also . . . not me? *Ask me anything you want to know and I will answer.* A question appeared. The question I had been asking in some form or another on all of my journeys.

"Is my mom okay?"

I answered myself immediately, but it was, again, not

me answering. *I'm happy. The living think the dead are suffering. We're happy. It's you all who are suffering. Not us. We're okay.*

I walked over and lay down next to my friend Elizabeth, whose parents had passed within a year of each other and who'd come with me seeking answers in the bowels of Van Nuys. She was crying. I took her hand as, thanks to Heidi, I was now comfortable doing and she turned to me. Her eyes were shining.

"Case," she said. "My parents are okay."

We had both received the same message. From within ourselves. A message so comforting, whether it's true or not (and I think you know I believe it's true) I considered myself finally healed. By the greatest healer of them all. Me.

Expect a miracle indeed.

Hiked Out

Yesterday, when I walked into my older son's playroom he and his best pal didn't even look up. They were deeply invested in the game they had made up. "Can I play?" I asked (halfheartedly). "YES!" my son yelled. "Okay. You work at the front desk of the hotel and Oscar and I are going to call and order room service. But we also want to take a surfing lesson with Shane and a tennis lesson with Kendra. So book that for us. Then, we're gonna play Amazon and we'll bring in all the packages you ordered that come to the house every day. If we can carry them all."

Huh.

Had I really been doing so much online shopping that even my imaginary packages would be too heavy? Either way I was worried. He's five. And while he has never had a surfing lesson or a tennis lesson, my mind was racing. Was he turning into a brat? He seemed so gentle and sweet, but would he grow up to be the last thing this world needs, which is another entitled white man? Should we move out of LA and should I sell soaps by the side of the road? Could I check myself into their pretend hotel?

What has become increasingly clear is that my son is

having a very different childhood from my own. At his young age he has been places and seen things I didn't see until he did. While I certainly grew up in suburban comfort, my childhood vacations were not spent under the roof of a hotel that can have room service to your door in under an hour. In fact, they weren't spent under any roof at 'tall. The stars were our roof, because the Wilsons were campers.

I have no recollection of where we would camp. The only place that's coming to mind is the Oregon Trail, but maybe that's only a computer game I loved? I do have what feels like hundreds of memories of pounding metal tent stakes into the cold ground while the sun was setting and my dad was asking if we had seen my mom, who had wandered off moodily the moment we arrived and hadn't been heard from since. My brother, Fletcher, and I were never *not* wearing oversize garbage bags fashioned into raincoats as we gathered up sopping wet firewood in the pouring rain. I know, for a fact, that we never once went camping in sunny weather.

As soon as our tent was up, my dad would call urgently to us, "Case and Fletch, help me! I'm chasing the light!" as he began duct-taping his most prized possession—his "invention"—between two trees. His invention, which had no formal name, looked like a green canvas banner. He'd sewn multiple pockets and compartments all over both sides of it to "hold stuff you need when camping." Patent pending. Each compartment was sewn to size, intended to fit a very specific object. A pancake flipper compartment. Syrup compartment. Flashlight compartment. Water purifier compartment. Coca-Cola compartment(s), as my mom needed about six Cokes for a one-night stay. For those, he sewed on one of those vertical fabric shoe compartments you hang over the door in college—so most of the cans dragged on the ground and weighed the whole thing down. It looked like a frantic patchwork nightmare, but it was quite handy and ingenious, just like my dad. As he secured each side, he'd reassure us, "I was an Eagle Scout. I know knots." This would come out garbled, since he always had a flashlight in his mouth for light. "Damnit, now, help me, we got one minute. One minute 'til the sun sets! Where's your mom?!"

My mom would wander back to the campground after sunset, though the walk never seemed to have cleared her head. She didn't love camping and would sit quietly while we roasted s'mores, usually silent until a howl of pain emerged after my dad misjudged where her body was in space in relation to the fire and stumbled over her Birkenstocks.

When night fell, we all crawled into the medium-size tent and lay four side by side, like the grandparents in *Charlie and the Chocolate Factory.* If my dad had to get up to go to the bathroom he would always, upon return, again misjudge where our bodies ended and his began in the dark and essentially belly flop onto all of us, trying to get back into his sleeping bag.

The camping trip that sticks out the most in my jumble of memories is the one we took when I was ten and my brother was six, and our parents decided to kick it up a notch and spring for four airplane tickets to California to camp in the Sierra Nevada. We would be going with their dear college friends and their kids, none of whom Fletcher and I had ever met. The plan was to ride on horseback for FIVE HOURS into the Sierras with guides who would drop us off at a high-altitude campground in the middle of NOWHERE and leave us for two weeks, with only our Eagle Scout to protect us. My parents hadn't seen Lori and Jack in a while, and this trip, which had been in the works for over two years, was their chance to reconnect with old pals. But about three minutes after we all met and/ or reunited, I heard my mom say to my dad, "Jack's . . . changed." That didn't seem like a good sign.

While Lori was boring but friendly, something about Jack made me nervous right off the bat. He had a major edge. He resembled John Heard's character in *Big*—the handsome bully—in both his looks and his manner. My mom HATED bullies. In a vintage Kathy Wilson move she would immediately start to bully the bully. "Send 'em my way," I can hear her saying. "They won't know what hit 'em." I knew right away that Jack wasn't long for this world.

The first night, we slept at the foot of the mountain so we could leave at dawn the next morning. Our guides gathered us and asked to see everything we were bringing to make sure it adhered to weight limits and could be evenly spread out over the eight horses we would be taking up

the mountain for the, again, five-hour ride. Jack wanted
to bring two handles of whiskey. My mom wanted to bring
a twelve-pack of Coke. The guides wanted us to bring water. Tensions were high.

By the time we mounted the horses the next morning,
I felt very anxious both about the river we had to wade
across, which was thigh high on the horses we were riding, and about spending two weeks in the wilderness with
Jack.

Many hours later, we finally arrived at our campsite
and everyone but me helped set up camp. There was a
tiny river you could walk down to and fish, which was the
perfect place for me to pace back and forth, pretending I
was on a long, exhausting work call from vacation. Even
in my fantasy world I was always working. My son and
his friend could take a page.

By nightfall, Jack was drunk. He started snapping at
Lori and his kids while my dad set up his canvas banner.
He couldn't yell at my mom, as she had wandered off somewhere. My brother and I felt terrible for their kids, Irene
and Elaine, although I also felt a secret sense of relief that
my parents weren't the crazy ones for once. Just last week,
my mom had gotten in trouble with our minister for passing notes and talking at full volume during his sermon.
"Say something to keep my attention!" she had said in her
defense. Hard to argue with that. At a certain point it was
on him. But it was a *tad* rude to circulate a questionnaire
written on the back of the tithing envelope to her favorite

church friends, asking "Brunch after church? Check yes or no!" In this setting, though, my mom was the normal one. It felt exhilarating and made me feel superior.

After dinner, we all sat by the fire. Because it was so close to bedtime, Mom treated herself to a couple cans of you-know-what and Jack kept on drinking. The rest of us drank the Crystal Light Lori made from those little powder packets, since we were allowed only beverages that weighed nothing, and afterward we would brush our teeth with toothbrushes whose handles had been sawed off to reduce their weight.

Later, as the Morrisons and the Wilsons lay in their respective tents, all was quiet. Until we heard the sudden sound of Jack screaming at his wife. At first no one moved a muscle, and we just lay there, terrified. Then my mom elbowed my dad, hard. "Paul, go out there. Now. She needs help." My dad pulled on his jeans over the full-body long johns onesie he always wore camping and stepped out of the tent. He tried to calm Jack down to no avail.

My mom got out of her sleeping bag but didn't have to pull on any clothes, since she was already wearing her signature one-piece purple Speedo bathing suit and shorts, an outfit that transitions beautifully night to day and one a daughter can be exceptionally proud of when her mom wears it to school pickup. She ducked out and brought Irene and Elaine back into our tent and then headed back out to the fire. I knew her help might be a mixed blessing. Deescalating a fight wasn't one of my mom's strong suits. That night, whenever things would start to die down, we would hear, "You do not scare me. Let that sink in." Then more yelling. Then "You're an asshole, Jack, and we all know it. Even you know it. So just stop. Stop it."

In the morning we found a note from Jack on a piece of paper he'd speared lovingly into a log with a huge knife. It said simply, "Hiked out." He had taken two steaks and some matches and one of our water purifiers with him. He was gone baby gone. He'd left his family all alone on top of a mountain in the Sierra Nevada. Everyone was thrilled.

The rest of the trip is less clear in my mind, though we have numerous photos of my dad pretending to hang one-handed off of every rock he encountered, as though he were falling off a cliff. I do remember that we had a great time, once Jack left. As the trip wore on, my mom started referring to him as "the bully" to Fletcher and me, and then openly to Lori and the girls. Now that he was gone my mom and dad duked it out for their rightful place as "weirdest parent," while Lori knew her place was "woman with least discernible spark of life."

No one else seemed to be wondering what I was wondering nearly every second, which was: Did Jack get back alive? We had come up with four guides and eight horses because of the complex terrain, and he had just hiked out on foot without a map? We found out the answer on the last day of the trip, after we'd successfully made it off the mountain and driven to Lake Tahoe to spend two nights in relative luxury, i.e., camping on flat ground. Lori was driving me and Irene to the grocery store in her mini-van when we saw a pickup truck coming toward us. "It's

Daddy," Irene said. He pulled up, and he and Lori rolled down their windows. The conversation was brief and Pinter-esque:

JACK: I put up the storm windows.

LORI: I want a divorce.

And that was it for their marriage. "It broke them, Paul!" my mom said oddly cheerfully when we heard the news. "Your dream trip broke 'em!"

When our family wasn't camping and bearing witness to the crumbling of a union, we were driving cross-country in our Cutlass Sierra to see our grandparents. We would alternate holidays, so every Christmas break we would drive to either Kansas City or Pensacola, Florida.

Being in the car for that long with my family and whatever dog of ours who hadn't yet run away was, in a word, hell. My brother and I would physically antagonize each other most of the time. And while most parents would separate their kids or scream at them to stop, my dad would look at the clock and yell, "Annnnnnnnd this begins our two-minute fighting period! GOOOOO." And for the full two minutes, we would beat the shit out of each other. If one of us was getting truly hurt, my mom would cry out, "Paul, stop, make them stop!" And my dad would say, "Kathy, you KNOW I can't stop them during the formal fighting period. It's out of my hands." It was a long two minutes.

On the road we would stop at seemingly every Mc-
Donald's we saw, and we were allowed to get whatever we
wanted because we were having what my mother called
"a big ol' time." And we were. For the first half of the trip.
Then, inevitably, the lights would go out.

WITHOUT FAIL, my parents would get into some ar-
gument and my mom would end up walking alone along
the side of the highway. This was such a common sight I
would barely look up from my Baby-Sitter's Club book.
My dad would inch alongside her as cars WHIZZED by
us, window open, pleading, "Kath, come on. Get back in
the car. We're on the highway, I can't go this slow." And
my mom would retort, "That's your problem, not mine!"
Usually these fights were triggered by a lifelong "disease"
my entire family suffers from: low blood sugar. This is not
a disease, but my parents raised us to believe a lot of bad
behavior could be blamed on it. "Anything can be solved
by a bag of nuts," my dad would say. He's not wrong. When
she got too cold my mom would finally get back in the car
and dinner at TGI Friday's or Cracker Barrel would lift
our spirits and soon my parents would be belting out "Ce-
celia" or "Only the Good Die Young." After singing the
latter refrain joyfully from the top of her lungs, my mom
would start to cry, and she would shake her head gravely
and turn back to us and say, "It's true. It's just *true*."

That was the predictable pattern of our drives, one exception being the time my dad attached a Sears brand
car top carrier containing all of our Christmas presents
and, inexplicably, all of my mom's clothes and her prized

fur coat, to the roof with seventeen bungee cords and cables and masking tape. As we drove to Missouri in heavy snow at dusk it flew off the car and into an embankment on the highway.

My mom immediately started screaming that my dad hadn't tied it correctly, which put him over the edge. As he pulled off at the nearest exit he exploded with an "I KNOW MY KNOTS!!!!!"

We never found it. In the ten minutes it took us to turn around and get back on the highway, someone had taken it. Stolen Christmas and stolen all my mother's clothes. She did have her purple swimsuit on her person, which was a relief, but my mom was the type of person who started shopping for thoughtful and personal Christmas gifts in January. And she was devastated. At the best of times, she was rarely spotted on the ground floor of my aunt Ann's house in Kansas City, but when we got there this time she immediately came down with bronchitis and took to the bed in Ann's third-floor attic. The "car top incident of 1991" had done her in.

On Christmas Eve, my dad and I frantically shopped for new presents. Though my parents had already spent the money they had budgeted for Christmas presents, my dad decided, fuck it, we are gonna make this holiday happen. So we repurchased a bowling ball for my brother and a Casio keyboard for me, which I told him we didn't need to wrap. "Maybe insurance will cover this," he kept wondering aloud. As we pulled back up to the house with the gifts, my aunt ran out to the front lawn and announced,

"The car top carrier's been found! A truck driver picked it up and was looking for you guys but never found you. He's in Minnesota now, but he can meet you in Charleston, West Virginia, in three weeks." We looked down at the bags in our hands. Tough timing.

As my dad's business grew and my mom transitioned out of politics, our family's money worries lessened. We moved to a nicer house and we went camping less and less often. In fact, one year my parents announced that for our annual vacation they were taking us to . . . CLUB MED!!!!!!

I hadn't heard of it, but my parents seemed thrilled. My mom said she was finally going to learn how to scuba dive, something my dad, brother, and I had gotten into in recent years. Even though she said she preferred to spend her tropical vacations watching *Seinfeld* reruns in the hotel room or lounging in the hot tub, I think she felt a little left out every time we would skip off for six hours to scuba. Which we would do multiple times because the three of us absolutely loved it. We were obsessed.

But when we arrived in Turks and Caicos, Fletcher and I were horrified to learn my mom had accidentally booked us at Club Med Singles. There were family Club Meds, we learned, and then there were eighteen-and-up Club Meds, where adults could do bad all by themselves without having to see or hear kids. Definitely not a sixteen-year-old girl and her thirteen-year-old brother. We had flown all the way there only to be informed at the front desk that kids weren't allowed. My parents pleaded with the manger and in a horrifying twist, he let us stay.

The first night we attended a cheesy "live show" put on by the staff, which was illuminated by tiki torches and fueled by Jell-O shots. They asked for volunteers from the audience, and my dad stood up and waved his hands like he was stranded on a boat trying to get the attention of a rescue helicopter. My mom put her head in her hands, and with good reason. Five minutes later, he was onstage, wearing a doctor's coat and stethoscope and high-kicking and karate-chopping to "Kung Fu Fighting." His performance earned him rave reviews and a standing ovation, and for the entire rest of the week, other guests sent shots over to "The Doctor."

"I love it here! I'm like, famous!" he told us the next morning (and every morning after). True to her word, my mom took her first scuba lesson after breakfast. We had reason to be apprehensive. She hated being told what to do and sports in general. (The exception being when she and her friend Lorraine volunteered to coach my five-year-old brother's soccer team, having never seen one soccer game in their lives. They each blew their whistles five hundred times per game and had the kids running in the wrong direction.)

But there she was, doing it! My brother and dad and I watched her lesson from the beach, cheering her on from a distance. My dad was especially happy she was taking the plunge, since he's a real "everybody has to at least try" kind of guy. And a "walk it off" guy. He carried a bat and ball and a *home plate* in his trunk in case we were ever over at a friend's house for dinner and our friend didn't know how to swing. We would look out the window and see him making a miserable kid choke up on the bat. No one asked him to do this. It was humiliating.

The three of us watched my mom struggle for twenty minutes to get her flippers on with all her equipment on her back in the Sha Sha Sha Sha Sha Sha Sha Sha-all-ows of the ocean. Her female instructor was very bubbly and full of energy, which seemed to anger my mom in the face of her own difficulties. While she practiced getting water out of her mask, the instructor was "too encouraging," and that was it. My mom stormed off, out of the ocean. It was a tough storm-off, though, because the second the oxygen tank surfaced from the water it weighed a million pounds and dragged my mom back in. She fell backward, but God love her, she got back up and continued the slowest, most labored dramatic exit I've ever seen.

Years later we would be scuba diving again, this time in Belize, on our first trip since my mom died. I'd brought my new boyfriend Paul along. Paul is a gifted comedian and one of the kindest people the world has ever produced, but scuba diving would not be his strong suit. Here we were again, in the ocean, the smug and already-certified Wilsons with a newbie in our midst. Paul had said up front he really had no interest in getting certified, but that wasn't gonna fly with Paul Wilson. So my Paul (this is your reminder that I have had two long-term boyfriends named Paul, same as my father) begrudgingly gave it his best shot.

He spent the first four days of his only vacation that year taking lessons in the small hotel pool while we had fun in the sun without him. By the fifth day, he only had one lesson left. And it was a test. The open-water dive.

We all set sail on a boat together out to a remote diving spot called Tackle Box, having decided that my family would be doing a more advanced dive while Paul and his instructor did their thing. The boat was SWAYING back and forth. "The sea, she's angry!" I said in a Scottish accent. I looked at Paul, who wasn't laughing at all. He looked seasick.

Most scuba divers get into the ocean by standing on the edge of the boat and falling off backward into the water. When he heard this, Paul looked like he was going to pass out. He chose to take the small metal stairs on the side of the boat, and we wished him well before heading down. The next time we saw him he would be certified! Our dive took about half an hour, and when we resurfaced Paul and his instructor were still underwater. Good sign. We climbed back on the boat, de-wet-suited, and made small talk with an older guy who told us he was a doctor. "I'm also a doctor," my dad lied. I don't recall if I said much to our other companion: LORI. The same Lori we went camping with in the Sierra Nevada, who was now DATING MY FATHER.

Finally, Paul's cute little head bobbed to the surface

and we all cheered wildly. He'd done it! He was water safe! Scuba Ready! My dad said, cupping his hands over his mouth so his voice would reach Paul in the water, "Isn't it transcendent? Casey and Fletch and I just love it. Meditative." But when the instructor had to hoist Paul over the side of the boat, we saw that something had gone terribly wrong. He was pale and nauseated and shivering and crying and snotting everywhere.

"Does he have the bends????" I screamed.

The instructor shook his head. "I think he's having a panic attack."

I was furious with my father. "You idiot! He didn't want to do this. He did this to please you! To impress YOU!" I turned to the doctor we had just met. "Can you do something?!" The doctor rushed to Paul and then—this is the only word for it—*cradled* him in his arms. Paul's fingers were now seizing up, creating what even he would later describe as "claw hands." He was drooling. We all crowded around him, telling him he would be okay, and then he started, most unfortunately, farting. We gave him some room.

Back on dry land, Paul had calmed down and the two of us sat on the beach wrapped in towels and drinking Gatorade. "I'm so sorry," I told him. "My dad's so frustrating. You don't need to ever scuba again." Paul was embarrassed but was a great sport as always. By dinner he was laughing about his ill-fated dive, and my dad gave him a weird trophy he'd walked into town to buy.

We moved on and after dinner, we decided to try the

local carnival. It didn't look exactly professional—in fact, it looked quite homemade—but its charming, swaying Ferris wheel looked like it got up to stuff, speed-wise. We all decided to try it.

We rode in pairs: my dad and Lori, sigh, Paul and me, and Fletcher and the doctor (no vacation friend left behind!). The ride started up and she whipped and she neighed. I was just starting to get a little scared when I noticed Paul's hands on the bar had started to . . . claw. Again. The drooling had recommenced. "Let me off!!!" he yelled to the bored seventeen-year-old running the ride, who was looking at his cell phone. I yelled to my dad to get the guy's attention and my dad craned his neck up to see us. "IS HE CLAWING *AGAIN*??!!" Each time we whipped around and passed the operator, my dad and I tried to get his attention, but it was moving so fast we could only get a quick word out before we zoomed past, a "Hey buddy!!," "Stop the," "Can you please," or "STOPPPPPP!" Finally, he heard us and paused the ride, but of course Paul and I were stuck on the top, swaying in the Caribbean breeze. You could hear the scrape of metal as our little car swung back and forth, back and forth. My boyfriend was having a full-blown meltdown now. My dad kept looking up at us in horror from the car right below us and then at me like "What the fuck's wrong with this kid??" The wheel finally moved forward so that we could get off, and in an image that is seared onto my brain, he ran at top speed away from me and the Ferris wheel into an open field and got down on his knees as if in prayer. Breathing heavily.

Away from the Wilsons. "The Wilsons will push you to the brink," my stepmom (NOT Lori, thank G) would later say. And my stepmom would be right. My dad turned to me, still in shock, and said, "It was a friggin' Ferris wheel! Again?!"

Years later still, we would go on our final scuba trip. My mom had been gone maybe eight years by then, and Paul and I had broken up, and my dad wanted to take us somewhere my brother had chosen for once. Fletcher loves learning, so naturally we went to the Galapagos Islands, the vacation equivalent of a science experiment, ugh. Diving there was only a problem in that the water was ice cold and dark and neither my dad nor I could get our wet suits on.

My brother said a piece of him died in one moment on that rickety boat in the middle of whatever body of water we were in. I had finally managed to get my wet suit on, but it was backward and had gotten wet, so I couldn't get it off by myself to turn it around, and I'd unfortunately forgotten to wear a swimsuit underneath it, so Fletcher had to peel the wet suit off my naked body inch by inch. My dad's wet suit was unfortunately a size or two too small, and my brother and I had to peel it off him together, both of us yanking on one arm as he bobbed back and forth between us like Danny DeVito as the Penguin in *Batman Returns*. Once we were finally underwater, about seventy-five feet below the surface, I happened to turn my head to the right to see that I was drifting toward the edge of a cavernous drop-off. My family was on my left, none the

wiser, and to my right I was being pulled toward an abyss
of utter darkness. I managed to swim back to them, but it
was bone chilling.

We haven't scuba-ed since. Maybe it's because my
dad's getting older, or my husband refuses to succumb to
Paul's fate ("I stand in solidarity with Paul. Now and forever," David says). Or maybe it's because we have kids. Or
maybe it's because whenever we would do it after my mom
died, we felt guilty. Like we were leaving her out again.
More than she was already being left out of our lives.

That trip to the Galapagos marked the end of a mourning period. The end of us as a threesome, mourning the
end of us as a foursome. All three of us would get engaged
that year, forging new families who would go on their own
vacations. As happy as our spouses and kids make us, I
get the sense now that we all sort of feel left out of being
a Wilson.

But I like to think of us, Fletcher and my dad and me,
weightless, floating underwater, no abyss in sight, mar-
veling at all we see ahead. Separate but together.

The BBQ

Old friends from college invited us over: June and Paul, Matt and Daryll, me and my old boyfriend Paul. It had been twelve years since graduation, and they wanted us to see their house and meet their kids. Catch up. Shoot the shit. Reminisce.

We had all been in acting conservatory together and had known each other for months upon years. Connor, our host, was a nice enough guy, but a cocky/nice in that white male privileged way white male privileged guys can be when they grow up in Brentwood and their parents are rich and liberal. He had a huge passion for acting but unfortunately his passion was accompanied by little talent. Luckily, time had fuzzied him up a bit. Life had knocked him around enough to take the edge off. And he meant well.

His wife, Larissa, on the other hand, had huge amounts of talent. She was a very pleasant, bubbly brunette who adored Connor. "She acts like she's won the lottery," I'd whispered to my friends the last time I saw them, probably four years prior.

Connor had actually been the one asking us over for

months upon years. Begging really, if I'm being honest. And we all had put it off as long as we could, until we received an email with the subject line: "ANY NIGHT IN MARCH WORKS!!!"

We went.

They lived deep in Valencia, in the shadow of Six Flags. We pulled up to a cute house with a sweet porch that I couldn't help noticing was covered with moving boxes. Every inch of it. After the six of us negotiated our way to the door and knocked, we were greeted by Larissa, who looked both frantic and annoyed.

"We're in the middle of moving," she said as her opener, as though we had STORMED the home, demanding a barbecue be thrown in our honor. She turned over her shoulder and screamed, "CONNOR! THEY'RE HERE!"

We all hesitated. I leaned in for a misguided hug. "Great to see you! Is this not a good time?" I asked, somewhat hoping she would say "You know what? Honestly it's not." And we would get to ease on down the road to El Compadre and enjoy well-done fajitas and flaming margaritas, as God intended.

Instead, she let us in and then delivered a doozy of a hostess line: "We don't have any food. Just Tylenol."

Huh. We did the math. No food meant someone would have to go get the food, bag the food, drive the food home, un-bag the food, and cook the food, before we could even start to eat the food. How long was this night going to last?

"I'll take some Tylenol," I said, brightly.

Connor appeared in the front hall, rumpled and exhausted, but gracious and excited to see us. "Let's take this party outside!"

We took the nonparty out to the dimly lit back deck. The sun had set and it was quite cold out, and every available seat was covered with wet leaves. Connor shut the sliding door behind him and looked embarrassed. "So sorry, guys, we're in a little bit of a . . . not a fight or anything but a little disagreement, sort of."

"Well, that's clear," June said.

I began to admire, deeply, the fact that our hosts didn't seem to give one single solitary fuckles in the world about our comfort as guests. Was this another by-product of growing up rich? The freedom to think us peasants don't even need to be fed or have our eyeballs rest upon anything aesthetically pleasing or deserve to sit upon dry wood?

"Larissa's gone to the store," Connor said.

We nodded.

"Good. That's . . . good for her," Matt offered, kindly.

Connor made a face. "I just hope she goes somewhere close and not to the Whole Foods over the hill." He stared off in a reverie. "She loves that Whole Foods." He walked over to the grill and made another face. "Shit. I gotta call her and tell her we need some charcoal, too."

"I haven't left yet."

We all jumped. Larissa had soundlessly opened the sliding door and was standing in the threshold, in terrifying silhouette.

"Connor," she said in a low, even tone. "I can't find the credit card. Did you pack it??"

"No," he said, affecting the same tone. "Why would I have packed it?"

"I don't know but I can't find it," she said through clenched teeth.

Something (else) odd was happening.

THE credit card? IT?? After college Connor's parents gave him ten thousand dollars to direct and produce a piss-poor production of *Three Sisters* I'd starred in, alongside Larissa. And now they had only ONE credit card??

We all had the same thought. He'd been cut off.

Her nostrils flared but she sustained her calm, chilling tone. "Can. you. at. least. help. me. look. for. it??"

We all instinctively began brushing the wet leaves off the patio furniture and settling in.

Connor looked increasingly annoyed. "I can't help you right now, Lariss, I'm trying to host my friends." He turned back to us. "Do you guys want anything, by the way? Wine or diet root beer maybe?"

I raised my hand. "I'd love a—"

"Fine," Larissa said, a threat in her voice. "Then I'll just have to get the other one."

"Stop," Connor warned her, deadly serious. "Don't. Just look for it, it's probably still in your purse from when you went shopping yesterday and somehow got no food."

"I'm *getting* the other one," she said with finality.

Larissa stalked inside, and through the kitchen window we could see her rummaging through the drawers and cabinets.

"What are you guys working on?" Connor asked.

"Um, this and that," Paul said. "I'm thinking about doing an animated show but who knows, it's sort of just an idea at this point . . ." He trailed off.

Larissa was back and she was holding a hammer.

"Larissa," Connor pleaded. "Come on. There's probably cash in my jeans pocket."

"I CHECKED THEM, CONNOR. THERE ISN'T!"

She then walked calmly across the deck and toward the grill and opened the door of a minifreezer I hadn't noticed. She pulled out a huge block of ice and rested it on the bench next to her. She began hammering away at it. Pieces went flying into the air. Matt and Daryll, the closest to her, politely turned away. After about a minute she pulled out a sopping wet credit card.

She held it up and looked at us as if to say "Happy now?" Or, "This is my life now. My private hell. You're welcome."

Here we were. Trapped outside, inside this unhappy marriage. A long way from college. A long way from *Three Sisters*. A long way from the rehearsal rooms on Lafayette Street we spent four years dreaming and scheming in.

Larissa wiped the credit card off on her shirt and walked back inside. The door slammed behind her. My mind flashed on so many fights my parents had had (they never shied away from a public disagreement) and a familiar fearful feeling washed over me. I had to get out of there.

But I didn't go. Because I wasn't eight years old. I was thirty.

I stood up and followed Larissa into the house and offered her some of her Tylenol. Happy I was staying for dinner, but relieved that at the end of the night, I got to go home.

Tears of
a Clown

I've had the pleasure of seeing some truly incredible theatrical performances in my life. I saw Patti LuPone play Mama Rose in *Gypsy*. Denzel Washington in *A Raisin in the Sun*. Lisa Rinna in *Chicago*.

And I've been lucky enough to perform with some of the all-time greats. Catherine O'Hara in *For Your Consideration*. Don Cheadle in *Black Monday*. Lisa Rinna in *The Hotwives of Orlando*.

However, hands down, the greatest performance I have ever seen was in a black box theater in LA on Santa Monica Boulevard. This is not usually where one goes to see dynamic theater, but rather where dreams go to die.

It didn't start out well. My boyfriend and I were there to see a production put on by friends of friends and they were serviceable, but the space was very cramped and it was extremely hot. The play was *not* a comedy. In fact, it was quite serious. The director sat above us on a plank, her legs swinging directly over our heads, which was unnerving. Again, this was very much not a comedy and it was very, very hot.

By intermission, I was ready to leave. But my boyfriend pointed out there were only ten of us in the audience and were we to go, the fact that 20 percent of the audience had skipped out would be both extremely obvious and a blow to the actors.

I knew what the actors were going through because I have been in some terrible theatrical productions myself. In college, I was in a performance of *Much Ado About Nothing* that was so bad, the head of acting said ALOUD to the audience, like a Greek chorus no one asked for, "We're in hell." It didn't feel good to hear that from onstage and have to continue trotting around on all fours because I was playing Dogberry as an actual dog. #Choices!

During an agent showcase, where you are performing specifically for agents in the hopes that they will see your face and pluck you from the multitudes, I made the choice to do a scene in which I had been kidnapped and the kidnapper had put a paper bag over my head. I had two minutes to make an impression and I chose to use one minute and fifty-seven seconds of that time with a Vons bag obscuring my face.

He was right. We had to stay. I sat down and settled in for the long haul. I could feel the director's dirty Birkenstocks brush the top of my head. She was literally watching us watch it, which annoyed me, because I hate when directors are in the audience doing their own performance of "director." It felt like undue pressure to respond stirringly to what was, sadly, a bad play. It was a lot of masters to serve.

But what was done was done. I made peace with the fact that the next hour of my life would be a wash.

And then it happened.

A man appeared on the street outside the barred window behind the actors, which was the literal backdrop of the black box, and looked into the room. He was a bit unkempt. His hair was wild beneath what appeared to be a collapsed brown top hat.

He checked out the onstage proceedings like a curious spectator and then turned and looked directly at the audience. Taking us in. For longer than felt comfortable. We stared right back, holding our breath, unsure of what was to come. I heard the director make a small sound, sort of a frustrated sigh. The play wasn't going well, and now we had company. The actors kept right on going, oblivious. We were nearing the emotional height of the play. It was getting tense—how long was he going to just stand there? Would he go? The answer became obvious. No. No, he would not be going. He would be staying. And what he did next, hand to God, was so wonderfully inspired and transformational it elevated not just this bad play but also life itself.

He began to perform in the window. It was as if after watching for a few seconds he determined the actors needed him. I certainly did.

First it was kid stuff, pulling a few faces. Then he pretended he was singing at the top of his lungs when it was obvious no sound was coming out. I burst out laughing. My boyfriend elbowed me, hard. No. The ten of us in the audience made an unspoken pact. For the actors' sake, we had to collectively pretend this wasn't happening.

He seemed to realize he needed to go further if he was gonna get this crowd. Onstage, the yelling and furrowing of brows continued, but on the stage outside, a man holding a forty-ounce malt liquor bottle began to do some space work.

He walked away. Beat. Then popped his head back in the window. Amazing. Then he disappeared for a little longer, prompting our adrenaline to rise—was he really gone this time? Had he forgotten about his obligation to the theater? He popped in again. Expressionless face and priceless positioning in the window. I heard a couple giggles.

I want to make it incredibly clear the laughter we were trying to hold back was not at this man's expense. Quite the contrary. A genuinely gifted comedian was in our midst, but as the Real Housewives say whenever anybody says anything, "It simply wasn't the time or the place."

Except for that it was. Outside the window, his work was getting avant-garde.

He LOWERED HIMSELF out of the window frame. A genius heightening for what was such a cramped stage. Beat.

Then we just saw the tippy-top of his top hat *slowly* ascend back into the window frame. Our clown was back.

People were outright laughing now. The actors noticed. He had us. He stepped to the left of the window and slowly reached *just* his forty-bottle back into the middle of the pane. He shook it at us, like a puppet. Then made a large circle in the air with it. Then reversed the circle. Then he crawled under the window to the other side, whipping the forty out of frame stage left, the opposite way from which it had entered. He did diagonal reveals. He got on his knees and rested just his chin on the ledge of the window. The actors attempted to barrel ahead. I didn't even have to turn around to feel the director melting down above me.

Then he treated us to a dramatic moment. He stood up and faced away from us, frozen for over a minute.

Then he abruptly walked away from the window, and his body grew fainter and fainter. He was now in the street. Then he looked back at us, over his shoulder, and winked. No one could hold it in any longer, and we exploded into laughter.

He crossed the street, raising his bottle as his staff, stopping traffic like Moses parting the seas. But he hadn't forgotten about us. He had merely enlarged his playing space. Cars honked. He kept them at bay. Then sprinted back to us and smushed his face directly against the window. Perfect.

The actors stopped altogether. There was no competing with him. He now stood about a foot back from the window, exactly the way he began. He started making exaggerated expressions that almost resembled commedia dell'arte masks. He was angry. Then joyful. Then sad. The tears of a clown.

I remember thinking, *Please let this moment never end, let him never take his bow.* (When it came, it consisted of him abruptly wandering off.)

I've revisited this performance piece so often over the years in my mind. I have never laughed so hard as I did that evening, when a bright light appeared out of nowhere and shared his immense talents. He will most likely not be in any agent showcase or make it to Broadway. But as Mama Rose sings at the end of *Gypsy*:

Some people got it and make it pay.
Some people can't even give it away.

He had *it*. And that night he gave us the play we needed to see. It wasn't the play we had paid for and his name and bio weren't in the program.

But he was the star of the show.

Happy
Endings

I got cast in the TV show *Happy Endings* during the unhappiest time of my life. Now, I know you're thinking:
man, this girl's got a lot of unhappiest times. But I *swear*
this time is up there with the worst. Down there with the
worst? The point is, it was bad.

My contract had not been renewed at *SNL*, but they
had at least returned my things. An intern had packed
them all into a huge box that arrived at my apartment in
LA so wet it nearly buckled under the moisture. I opened
the box and it was full of my trinkets and good-luck charms
and this beautiful black-and-white photo of my mom.
Everything was smashed into a zillion pieces and about
eight bottles of alcohol we'd been given by the various
hosts had broken because the intern hadn't bothered to
add a stitch of bubble wrap. Which is a step I would have
skipped as well, so I couldn't fault him or her, but . . . still.
The contents of the box looked like my entire experience
on *SNL*: a mess of shards with my mom at the bottom of

it all. She'd just passed when I booked the show, and now here she was, smiling, with Ben Affleck's bourbon and melted Godiva chocolates all over her face. I mean I'm sure she liked Godivas, but not that much.

It was now pilot season, a three-month hellscape from January to March in which actors of all age, stripe, and creed audition for every possible upcoming network TV show and pray to win the acting and financial lottery— aka, a role as a series regular. (Then cable took over and it became year-round desperation.) But this year was even more important. Crucial. I was DETERMINED, privately (to a level that made me scared of myself), to book a pilot. To show everyone (?) some people (?) myself (?) that I would not simply be a two-season-and-done forgotten *SNL* cast member, put to pasture like the wig molds of my head that were housed somewhere in the bowels of 30 Rock. Lots of people who are fired from *SNL* fade away, poof, and I WASN'T GOING TO GO DOWN LIKE ALL THAT.

No, I vowed, with terrifying intensity, I would book *something*. Anything. Friend of the friend of the friend! I'd be anyone's friend! I'd be a passing acquaintance of the main character. A stranger to the main character who we never really get to know or see. A disembodied voice-over that illuminates something for the main character but has the potential to be cut, because why do we even need that voice-over, really? I'd take it. It was all I thought about. Tortured myself over. This was not a period in my life when I "showed self-compassion and self-love and talked to myself like I was my six-year-old, innocent, child-of-

God self." No. That never lights a fire in my fanny. Instead, I said cozy things to myself like, "You better get
another job, you fucking fat talent-less fuck."

It was not a "joyful time."

But in the mean and between time, I would find comfort in a little ole show called *Keeping Up with the Kardashians.* And would proceed to keep up with every. last.
one. of. them. to. this. very. day.

I loved Kris. I connected with her so deeply, and I
was so INTO the show I felt like I was her sixth daughter
(Kasey, obviously). I wanted Kris in my life. To comfort
me and lift me up and push my career forward with the
tenacity of a woman who may or may not have leaked her
second-oldest daughter's sex tape. Now THAT was the
kind of loving, supportive mother I needed.

I blew through twelve seasons in three months, and
by the end of March the writing was on the wall for my
career.

I had been on twenty-seven auditions and booked
zingo. My manager, Naomi, told me there were simply no
more shows to audition for. I felt utter shame and self-
loathing. The same way Kim must have felt when she divorced Kris Humphries after her divorce from Damon
Thomas. Like I had failed twice.

I WAS, however, offered a fun part as a rich basic bitch
on my friend Nick Kroll and Jon Daly's pilot presenta-
tion for Comedy Central, *Rich Dicks*, which would later
become the brilliant *Kroll Show.* Because it was just a pre-
sentation, it meant it'd be one day of work for the actors,

and then Comedy Central would decide if they liked it enough to shoot the real pilot. A pilot of the pilot. But I was so happy and grateful to Nick and Jon (and still am). I remember driving up steep, windy canyon roads to the house where we were shooting, awash in gratitude. While I knew this wasn't the job that would signal to our industry and my dad that I wasn't just another *SNL* refugee—it was a start.

And then, midhair and makeup, Naomi called and informed me there was *one* train, a little engine that could, that hadn't left the station. A pilot called *Happy Endings*, a sitcom about six friends in Chicago, written by a first-time writer, David Caspe, had been greenlit late in the game. The thing was, they had been seeing girls all week and the last audition was . . . today. They were testing two girls for the president of ABC at noon who were their first and second choices, but if I could get there in an hour, they would see me. I would have to leave immediately and drive across town to Sony if I wanted to read for it. "There's no way I can go," I told her. "I'm literally sitting in hair and makeup for Nick's show. My friend who has given me a huge opportunity." I hung up the phone and told myself it wouldn't have worked out anyways. The phone rang again. It was my other manager, Brooke Pobjoy, whose first and last name I will use because this second phone call changed my life.

"You have to go. This one's funny."

I staggered like a zombie over to where Nick was ABOUT TO SHOOT, and pulled him aside with tears in

my eyes and asked him if I could run out really fast—
just a quick three-hour-and-change round-trip. He was
stunned. And then he inexplicably said, "Go. We'll film
around you and do your stuff when you get back." Hero.
Angel. Mensch.

I drove to Sony with my hair sopping wet, no makeup
on my face, and without having read the script, let alone
memorized a single line of dialogue. For any other audition, I would know my lines cold. All I knew was that I
was reading for a role named Penny, and she was a train
wreck. Perfect.

Once in the room, I tried my best, but it was veryyyyy
obvious that I was reading the lines aloud for the first
time. David Caspe was there, and I noticed right away
how warm and friendly he was, so I relaxed a bit. David
was seated next to the man I refer to as "the most normal
man in Hollywood," co-showrunner and heart of a human, Jonathan Groff (not the JG of *Frozen* fame). Sitting
in front of them were the Russo Brothers (later of Marvel
fame), who were directing the pilot, and producing legend
Jamie Tarses. They all laughed a lot, but most of the time
when they laugh it actually means you don't get the part.

I thanked them and was walking out and down the
steps when Anthony Russo caught up to me. Could I be at
the network test? "It's in an hour," he told me. "And could
you maybe, um . . . dry your hair and learn the lines?"

Another phone call to Nick and I was soon auditioning against two of my hilarious pals for the role. Afterward, I sprinted to my car and while winding back up the

canyon to set, I got the call that I'd been made a series regular on *Happy Endings*.

I was ecstatic on a level that, to this day, I have never come down from. I felt relief that the then–love of my life (acting) and I were back together. It was the biggest break of my life, much more so than *SNL,* actually. I always knew in a shadowy part of my heart that I wasn't meant to be on *SNL*. I felt like an impostor. It was slightly excruciating, like I was on a sports team but sat on the bench week after week, watching people do what I so desperately wanted to be doing. I felt like I had been invited to a party where everyone knows each other but the host doesn't bother introducing you. I'd pitched twenty-seven ideas for Weekend Update and wasn't allowed to do one. In my opinion, Weekend Update is sort of your introduction to America. Otherwise, longtime fans seem to get not just mad, but *angry* to see a new featured cast member wandering around in the margins of the show. And they expressed as much in comments online like "WHO THE FUCK IS THAT?????" and more lovingly, "She looks like Mike Myers swallowed a couch." So.

I also just didn't possess the skill set required to succeed there. I didn't really do impressions beyond Katy Perry and Jennifer Aniston and "Sleepy Norah Jones." The other cast members were *so* brilliant at them and at doing huge characters, and I felt like my style just didn't line up. Which was no fault of anyone! Lorne Michaels once told me "Good acting isn't rewarded here," which I thought was generous, given that it wasn't working out, and I appreciated hearing it. That's not to say the cast members aren't good actors—they are all absolutely genius actors in their roles outside of *SNL*. But sketch performing is different from acting, and the scenes I wrote were essentially always two women sitting at a bar and emotionally unpacking the nuances of their lives and the textures of their grief. Not necessarily . . . hilarious??

But now, a year later, I was playing the role of Penny Hartz on a show called *Happy Endings,* and it was clear in my bones that this was *my* part. Penny was desperate for love and initially written in a sharp but slightly cynical way, so I decided to play her with optimism because most of the amazing single women I knew who were looking for love were fun and genuinely hopeful. I connected to this thirsty and wildly over-the-top positive disaster of a human who said things like, "Uh, yeah. I did take a whore's bath last night. I had a one-night stand and didn't have time to shower. So did I rub some dryer sheets on my pits and splash some water on my hush in the bathroom of an Au Bon Pain? Yes, I did."

The first day of shooting the pilot, I met a comedic soul mate in Adam Pally. I'd known him a little from UCB in New York and always thought he was sweet and funny, but I didn't know he was also a wild man and a deviant—a word I mean as a compliment in this context.

We hit it off right away, soon feeling *incredibly* free to say things to each other you wouldn't say to your worst enemy. Too free, maybe. I tried telling him Lorne Michaels and I had always gotten along really well and that despite everything, I thought he'd really liked me. Adam looked at me deadly serious. "He hates you. You didn't deliver. He wouldn't have fired you if he liked you." Honest stuff. And I told Adam, just as meaningfully, about a week into filming that if he would JUST lose weight, he could be Matt Damon, but unfortunately it didn't "look like it was headed in that direction."

Adam was cast as Max Blum, a character named for my husband's dearest friend Max, who had tragically passed away the year before. Max Blum was a gay character who defied all stereotypes. He was a sloppy mess, lazy as hell, and as unkempt as could be. He was incredibly whiny, very nasty, hilarious and dry and mean and needy but ultimately a sweetheart and everything you hope to see in one character. A lot was on the page, but Adam brought so much complexity to it. His is one of my all-time favorite comedic performances, and one of the ones I find most moving, which isn't always the case in a sitcom. The character of Max touched a lot of people because his sexuality was nowhere near the focus of who he was. He was proud to be gay, but was also just as insane and selfish and rude as the rest of the characters.

Max's relationship to Penny also touched anyone who knew the deep, unshakable bond, as comforting and old as time, between the single gal and the gay best friend. Penny and Max were all at once siblings, soul mates, and frenemies. Alwaysssss up to stuff. For a Halloween episode we went as mommy and baby in a BabyBjörn, which required us to wear a harness for nineteen hours of filming (we were on the front lines!). Adam sat on a little wheeled scooter underneath my dress with just his head popping out of a hole under my breasts. Between takes he had no other choice than to lay his (huge) head upon my (huge) bosom while we would discuss and rank the attractiveness of various below-the-line crew members. "Below the line" refers to everyone but the actors and director. Sadly, we called everyone by their first name and position, as in "Alisha Props" or "Doug Sound Mixer." No one called us Casey Actress or Adam Actor, but everyone knows, as Adam would say, that "above the line can do whatever they want."

We *got* each other. During filming Adam lost his beloved mom, suddenly. We both witnessed the spirals of our dads as they trudged through grief, nearly drowning. He concussed me with a boom mic. I had to physically drag him away from a craps table in Vegas. Twice. Both times at 11:00 A.M. He emceed my wedding and rudely called it and the crowd of mostly actors a "Who's Who of Who's That?" I bore witness to his style evolution and escorted him to an Emmy party in which he wore Birkenstocks over lime-green socks to emulate Kanye West. He's yelled at journalists who asked dumb questions about the show and continues to stalk them online to this day. He will say or do ANYTHING. He lives on the edge. And that's a fun person to be around. You don't meet many people who will risk life and limb and dignity for a laugh. He is untethered in the greatest way, but no one is worried about him because he is also the nicest little mensch alive.

When I got bronchitis for two weeks, he checked in on me every day. Toward the end of that two weeks I sent him a text that said, "I WISH HAPPY ENDINGS HAD BEEN ON NETFLIX AND FOUND THE AUDIENCE SCHITT'S CREEK DID." To which he responded, "ANNNNND SHE'S BACK! I AM AT PEACE KNOWING YOU ARE FULLY JEALOUS AND RECOVERED." So many duos come up to me with a certain little glint in their eye and I can just tell from their energy what they're gonna say. "I'm the Penny. He's my Max." It warms my heart that Adam and I have each other and that Penny and Max had each other. Scarecrow, I think I'll miss you most of all.

Adam is not the only one I deeply miss. The show featured four other equally unhinged touchstones. Four other brilliantly funny and amazingly weird actors, playing equally amazingly weird roles.

Elisha Cuthbert, who was very famous in large part due to her starring role on 24, played Alex. Elisha is as pretty as a picture. A picture that opens its mouth to reveal a low Tallulah Bankhead husky voice with a foul mouth and a cig dangling from her perfect pout. (She's since quit.) She was even more beguiling a creature than you could imagine. And had been acting the longest. (I was right behind her, if you counted the one line I had in a movie with John Malkovich that was cut.) Elisha had been acting since she was a glint in her parents' eyes. We bonded immediately and she single-handedly taught me how to be on camera, dragging me subtly to my mark whenever I wasn't on it, which was always.

As "number one" on the call sheet, she took her role

very seriously. "Number one" means you are the star and therefore set the tone of the show, show up first, dictate the culture of the set, and set an example for how hard everyone would be working. She was a PRO. She explained that she had learned what it means to lead a cast from Kiefer Sutherland himself in *24*, and he didn't tolerate any guff, and Elisha tried her best to impress upon us we must know our lines and not have our phones out during takes and not show up late, something that no one listened to ever.

Elisha has an incredible sense of humor and was an absolute ball from day one. She was the only cast member with an actual home when we started, and she welcomed us over all the time. If we weren't there, we were hanging in her "living room," which is what she called the Chateau Marmont. This was all so new to me, as I normally ate in my car outside the Crunch Fitness on Sunset Boulevard. I felt so glamorous tooling around in Elisha's Porsche, listening to her stories and making her laugh. She is such a hard worker. So tenacious. So wonderfully self-deprecating. SO funny. And body be bangin'.

I'll never forget the episode where our characters wore "hair helmets." After a fall down a flight of stairs left Penny with a concussion, she had to wear a helmet for a month. Bummed that she would miss out on dates, Alex had the brilliant idea to glue a wig that looked exactly like Penny's hair to a bike helmet. She could stay safe and still look great. No one would be the wiser—except for the result being terrifying. In the episode where Penny finds out she can speak Italian when she's drunk, we drank so much orange juice as mimosas and Elisha ate so many racks of ribs we threw up for the rest of the day. Elisha was game for anything.

If anyone messed with any of us, she would set them straight right quick. I was both scared of her and in awe of her. Mama Bear we called her. She became so adept at comedy over the years it was astonishing. I love my little "Leesh Leesh" and learned so much from her. And later, when she was doing *The Ranch,* she invited me to the makeup trailer to meet my idol, Debra Winger, because that's the kind of friend she is. And then we went and had a drink in Elisha's living room.

Damon Wayans Jr. played Brad. There aren't enough words in the English language or stars in the sky to describe how I feel about my angel sent from heaven, Damon. He is the NICEST, most kindhearted, magnetic, charming, delightful, sweet, hilariously inappropriate (you can take the boy out of the Wayans Family, but you can't take the Wayans Family out of the boy) person I have ever met. EVERY SINGLE SECOND SPENT WITH HIM WAS PURE JOY. Utterly. I laughed so hard at him one night I singed my bangs on a nearby heat lamp.

His voices, his impressions, his observations, were spot-on. And he is so generous. For a cast and writers' trip to Vegas after season one wrapped, Damon rented us a party bus that had been thoughtfully outfitted with a stripper pole. Our fun ride turned into a hellish, eight-hour, traffic-filled journey in 104-degree heat. The rest of us arranged other transportation home, except for Damon, since as he said, "someone has to return it."

I've read many interviews in which actors say someone was so funny they made them "break." I never understood this. You have rehearsed and seen the sketch one hundred times by the time you do it. But with Damon, I finally got it. Filming the episode in which Brad and I kill Alex's racist parrot, Damon and I could not stop ruining takes. He made such funny little squeaks and sounds as reactions that when I saw him carrying the dead bird with tongs and then give the bird mouth to mouth, I truly could not handle it. My line was "What would Kerry Washington do? Demand to see the president and then make out with him." I could only say it once, as we were howling, with tears running down our faces. I wish I'd gotten to do more with Damon, but Penny and Brad were not a frequent pairing. The bird episode, though, along with watching Damon shoot the mini one-take musical number of Brad going to the dentist, was up there with the most fun I had on set.

Damon is a teddy bear and I'm going to say it, THE funniest person I've ever worked with. He has the gift. He's a star. My baby Damon.

Eliza Coupe played Jane. Eliza and I had also met in passing at UCB, and she was, and is, a force to be reckoned with. The best thing about Eliza is that she possesses my favorite quality in a human. She is wildly self-deprecating while at the same time being someone you take seriously. Hilarious, wild, ambitious, hardworking, totally and

wholeheartedly herself, silly and gorgeous and fascinat-
ingly complex, Eliza made us laugh endlessly. She also let
us make fun of her love of formal short shorts, her insane
nail colors, her passion for raw carrots, and her delightfully unhinged morning routine. I'll try and explain it
here, but find her and have her take you through it (she
will). You haven't lived until it's been documented for
you.

- Wake up.

- Dry brush the entire body.

- Tie the same old sweatshirt around waist that has been
  playing this role for years upon years in order to feel,
  quote, "held and secure."

- Turn on the coffeepot IN THE DARK to wake up the
  senses.

- Drink coffee at the dining room table, contemplating what
  the day might bring.

- Turn the lights on.

- Twenty minutes of light journaling.

- Thirty minutes of yoga.

- Twenty minutes of more lucid journaling.

- Blending of many turmerics and collagens and fish oils
  and supplements into smoothie(s).

- And lastly—and perhaps most meaningfully—"Stare out
  the window for a while."

She is a rare gem. And an incredibly sensitive and thoughtful one. One day I came into my trailer and found a gorgeous bouquet of flowers from her. "You mentioned a while back that today was your mom's birthday. Thinking of you." I hadn't remembered even telling her, or anyone, and her remembering and honoring my mom meant so much to me. I wish for one hour I could go back and witness her and Damon in between takes making each other collapse in laughter, in their own world as "husband and wife," building their incredible chemistry that everyone loved.

Zach Knighton, who played Dave, was the last one cast because it was a tricky role. Dave needed to be handsome, funny, smart, lovable, sensitive, the kind of guy every girl and guy would want to marry. And have sex with. And Zach was it! The minute he got the part, I started getting texts from female friends and strangers alike asking if I could maybe put in a good word for them with Zach?? Or telling me he had been in a class with them in college and to this day no one has struck them as more handsome and cool. And he was all of those things. He was the type of guy who would hop on his motorcycle at night and just see where the road took him. He's incredibly outdoorsy in the way, how shall I say, that many actors are not. He built his house with his bare hands. Adam and I once went to a party at his house in Venice, and were stopped in our tracks by the sight of two surfboards leaning effortlessly against the gate, a boat in the driveway and a camper behind it. We were not made of that stock. We were cold and it was eighty degrees. Zach was funny as hell and easy breezy to be around. I'll never forget the way he would saunter onto set with a coffee and a twinkle in his eye and say in this quiet baby voice, "Hiya, Case." He wasn't just a pretty face, however, and when the writers realized he could look like the straight leading man but venture much further afield comedically and be just as weird and dumb and embarrassing as the rest of the characters, they went for it. Zach's Dave started priding himself on his Deep Vs (verryyyyyy low V-neck T-shirts. Too low!) and fedoras, and Zach's brilliant character acting came forth.

We were all surprised when our little-show-that-could got picked up for a full season and then ran for three years. You have either seen *Happy Endings* and love it beyond measure (the fan base is equally rabid and furious it was canceled), or . . . you've simply never heard of. (PLUG: it's on Hulu.) There was just something special about it. An alchemy between the cast and the *incredibly* talented writers (most of them have gone on to create their own shows). It was silly and hard funny and good-natured and weird, filled with insane dialogue (all delivered at lightning speed) like Max's line (written by Matthew and Daniel Libman): "If Mary Tyler Moore married and then divorced Steven Tyler, then married and divorced Michael Moore, then got into a three-way lesbian marriage with Demi Moore and Mandy Moore, would she go by the name Mary Tyler Moore Tyler Moore Moore Moore?"

A year into filming, having polished off more than my share of male guest stars, I would start dating the aforementioned creator of the show, David Caspe.

We got together over the summer, and when we finally told the cast, we embarrassingly acted as though we were delivering some monumental news that would change the course of their lives forever.

"No one cares. We don't work at the U.N.," Adam told us. "And also, everyone already knew."

My husband is an absolutely brilliant, gifted, and inspired writer. I am so grateful to him for the role of Penny Hartz. And every role he has written for me since. He wrote *Marry Me* (another PLUG: on NBC) about our relationship, so I essentially played myself, and currently I'm on *Black Monday* (on Showtime, PLUGGGG), where I get to play Tiff, a rich, 80s Ivana Trump–esque, hell-on-wheels heiress to a denim fortune. Oddly Tiff is even less of a stretch than my character on *Marry Me*. Since day one, no one has believed in me more than David. And the fact that we get to spend our lives together and raise our baby boys together and on top of all that still get to collaborate creatively leaves me struggling for words. Meeting him is the single greatest thing that has ever happened to me. (Except for when Kris Jenner sent me a gift basket after I talked about her memwah, as she calls it, on *The Ellen DeGeneres Show*.)

Happy Endings allowed me to shuck off the professional insecurity that had plagued me post *SNL*. And I got to sing and dance at a boat show to Natalie Imbruglia's

"Torn" with my version of the Divine Miss M., Megan Mullally, who played my mom. I got a signature look—pajoveralls—and I even got a catchphrase! Amahzing! (Sorry.)

After the third season I was hopeful the show would return for another, but I also sensed it was our last. Which it ended up being. It didn't take time away from the show for me to finally feel the force of all that it meant to me. I didn't feel "in hindsight happiness," because I felt such intense gratitude and happiness *as* it was happening. It was a real loss. A loss of friendships. A loss of such a special time and place in all of our lives. Over these years, children were born, relationships began, marriages ended, parents were lost, life was lived. And deeply unexpected things happened, such as when production shut down because Adam's beautiful mom accidentally ate two pot cookies from his trailer, which he had gotten from "Gary Boom Operator." The assistant director had to pull Adam aside and tell him his mom was crawling around on all fours and didn't know who the president was. When an EMT asked her how she was feeling she said, "I'm feeling horizontal." I blame Adam for this.

The point is, *Happy Endings* saved me in so many ways. And I still miss it terribly. So terribly I could hardly write this. And yes, I REALIZE IT'S JUST A TV SHOW, and again, ONE THAT VERY FEW PEOPLE EVEN SAW—but that's okay. For me it was a sea change. A tectonic shift.

It's been eight years since the show ended, and I now

know the reason I was on it was much bigger than "proving *SNL* wrong." How exactly do I know that? A psychic told me, naturally. (I know I know I said I wouldn't see them anymore. And I didn't for a loooong time. I swear.) Laura Lynne Jackson—the only psychic whose brain has been studied by scientists, TAKE THAT—spoke with me and was eerily and immediately able to channel my mother. She said, "In 2005 you had a huge professional experience, huge, life-changing. But it ended early. Don't feel badly about that. Your mom keeps saying, 'We had to get you out of there.'"

I had to stop her. "I mean, I wish she had let me have a little more success before I left, maybe a recurring character or . . ."

"No," Laura, channeling my mom, responded. "We had to get you out of there in order for you to meet David. And have the boys."

You know how I want to end this essay. I want to end this essay with the name of the show. YOU KNOW I DO. YOU KNOW I SHOULD. THAT I CAN'T NOT. BUT THAT I PROBABLY SHOULDN'T BECAUSE IT'S TOO OBVIOUS.

And so, I'll end with a thank-you and a nod to our biggest fan, renowned TV journalist Damian Holbrook, who loved and embraced and got the show INSTANTLY. (The character of Damian from *Mean Girls* is inspired by him, it's worth noting.) Damian was our earliest champion and part of the reason the show got out there at all. He loves it so much he even got a tattoo on his forearm of the word *Happy* in the official show font. Bless him. But it's *another* tattoo of his that my mind returns to again and again when I think of *Happy Endings*.

I would always comment on it over the years when Damian would interview me, or we would run into each other. It's a tribute to his late mother—a phrase she used after she had a fantastic dinner, or after a perfect day, or when an experience was so meaningful it changed the course of her life.

"OH, DID WE ENJOY."

I love that. Oh, did we enjoy.

Indeed. We did.

My Husband's Just Not That into Me; or, Afrin: A Love Story

They say the key to a good marriage is marrying someone who likes you more than you like them.

I have not taken this advice. In fact, I've done the opposite. My husband would disagree, but in my heart of hearts I know where we stand. I like him more. And them's the facts, Jack.

If anything, unlike some relationships, which, post-kids, take a gradual or even drastic downward spiral, I'm a little embarrassed to admit I not only remain obsessed with my husband, but that the obsession is . . . growing.

So much so that, six years of marriage in, I feel I must continually work on gaming him into liking me. It was so hard to get him that I know better than to settle in and relax now that I have him. Can't stop won't stop.

Oddly enough his sister, Shira, is the one who gave me this advice: "Even when you're married, you have to keep wrestling for power. Don't call him too much. Let *him* call *you*. You're busy!"

"Right. Taking care of our kids and our lives on top of my job—" I respond.

She cuts me off. "Maybe! But maybe with other stuff. Who can say? You're a mystery."

My sister-in-law has a lot of advice to offer in the realm of maintaining the power in relationships, and I trust her implicitly. While some of it is questionable, damnit if it doesn't work. For instance, if you're in a new relationship and struggling to level the playing field and not seem so desperate, she advises the following: "At four P.M., your phone goes in a drawer. Preferably off. Take NyQuil. Full dose. Get in bed. Sleep. Wake up, turn on your phone, and delight in the texts that have gone UNRETURNED ALL NIGHT. Most likely the sender is in an emotional spiral and if you're lucky you'll have two to five texts, the last one being the pinnacle: 'ARE YOU OKAY??' To this you reply, 'GREAT!' And nothing else. This will put them further on their motherfucking heels. Also," she adds for good measure, "you will feel skinny, having skipped dinner. Win-win."

Again, some of it may be questionable so take what you need and leave the rest. Many have asked her what to do if they wake up at say, 3:00 A.M. Shira's response? "DOUBLE DOWN ON THE NYQUIL. You'll squeeze a little more power out of not responding 'til eleven A.M." She also strongly advises that EVEN IN LONG-TERM RELATIONSHIPS you should avoid asking questions in your texts. It's weak and it shifts the balance. Now you're left waiting for a response and you suddenly need something from them. Responses to their questions should be as short as possible. One word is preferable, no emojis. UNLESS THE ENTIRE RESPONSE CONSISTS OF ONE EMOJI. YOU ARE BUSY. YOU DON'T NEED THEM. IF ANYTHING, THEM TEXTING YOU IS A BOTHER.

This is the same person who recently mused, "Remember when we were young and thought love mattered?" She's an onion. IMPORTANT SIDEBAR: Shira has great parenting advice as well. "Buy real books, keep them close by, and when you hear your kids coming, pick them up and pretend to be reading to set a good example," she says. THE INTENTION HERE IS **NOT** TO REALLY READ THE BOOK. GOD NO. Shira believes we can get just as much bang for our buck as if we actually did the things we want them to see us modeling. She's a big fan of wearing workout clothes when you drop your kids off at school, making mention that you are headed directly to a workout class. You are most certainly not. But your kids don't need to know that. Brilliant. (Note to the reader: feel more than free never to read this book but just leave it lying around, ready to trick your kids at a moment's notice.)

I have attempted to follow Shira's advice. I try to bring certain issues to my therapist or my girlfriends so I don't put alllll my emotional needs on David. I try to act as aloof as one can when you're putting a crib together, together. I try to wait for him to call me. That's no easy feat, because we see each other every single morning and every single night and we work together most days on set. During the quarantine, keeping my distance and an air of mystery was really hard, given the fact we worked side by side from our bed. BUT IT'S NOT IMPOSSIBLE. I'd put on noise-canceling headphones and when he would ask me something I would take one side off and say, rudely, "What??" However, in normal times, I know from experience that if I don't call David during the hours we're apart, we will simply never speak.

I know this because this dynamic has been baked into the DNA of our relationship since day one. On a trip to Las Vegas with the *Happy Endings* cast to celebrate the end of our first season, I felt sure something was happening between us. Nothing had, but I found him very cute so I assumed the feelings were mutual. After he said good night to everyone, I sprinted after him and followed him to the elevator, where I stuck my foot in the door so it couldn't close. Although he had no choice, I was touched when he asked me if I wanted to come back to his room. We ended up kissing, and before I left he handed me a doodle he had done on the hotel stationery of a shark and the words, "Thanks for the Memories!" This was happening!!!!

When I didn't hear from him for a couple of agonizing weeks, I decided it was time to show him who was boss. I vowed I wouldn't communicate with him AT ALL unless he called me. Let him wonder where I was or who I was with or what I was doing. Three devastating months of silence later, I ran into him at a bar and he asked brightly, "How are you?" He had no idea we hadn't been talking.

A few months later we were still talking and hanging out, but he had yet to commit his life and eternity to me. I knew I had to make him jealous, so I slept with a well-known writer, and when that didn't work, I slept with a well-known director. Nothing. Finally, I pulled out the big guns and slept with a moderately well-known actor. The moment I let that slip, David asked me to go out, and we've been together ever since. THIS IS VERY SAD, I realize. But now you know why I feel I MUST maintain distance where I can. For my own dignity.

But it's hard. Because the truth is, I just really love talking to him. He's a doll. A lovely, generous, truly kind human. He's a supportive, hilarious, compassionate, moral, tall, dark, and handsome guy. And an incredible dad beloved by his children and by most people who meet him. I feel so incredibly lucky he chose me, I thank God every day that I made him go out with me.

When we first started dating exclusively, and he had finally retired the numbers of the hostesses of seemingly every restaurant in West Hollywood, I would feel a pang of loneliness so strong it alarmed me when he would leave my sight, even just to go to the bathroom. This really creeped him out then, but to this day, whenever he gets up from bed or exits a room—EVERY SINGLE TIME—I ask, "Where are you going?" "TO THE BATHROOM!!!!!" he yells, shocked that I am still sad to see him go.

I've told my friends that if something ever happens to him, they need to get to me *immediately* because I **will** end my own life and I have my children to think about. If they don't get there in time? That's on THEM.

And if I should die before him, I've told him in no uncertain terms that I will not be on the other side, "wanting him to be happy with someone else." If he does remarry, I will haunt him *and* her. And it will kill me AGAIN.

If we get divorced, make no mistake, there will be no "conscious uncoupling." There will be zero attempts to abide by this bizarre and insane trend of staying dear friends with your ex and vacationing together with your kids and your ex's new, younger girlfriend. NO THANK YA!!!! I love him so much that if we break up, we will hate each other and smear each other's good name in a very public custody case.

And so it is this mix of fear and love that runs like a river through our relationship. I'm not proud of this, but being away from him makes me feel like, in the words of Vicki Gunvalson from *The Real Housewives of Orange County,* "I need my love tank filled."

But I can't let him know that.

So, I've decided that besides our standard midday check-in about the kids and plans, I can't just call him to say "hi" like some loser. Too thirsty. Any additional call on top of the check-in needs to have a reason.

Those reasons vary. Sometimes I call pretending to have other "pressing" logistics to discuss. I try and ask a question that will win me points *and* serve to remind him that I am indispensable (which is, another sidebar, our main fight: how much I do for our family on top of working full-time. I try to weave that into every conversation we ever have).

An example of a "logistical" call:

ME: Hey. Are you booking the tickets to El Paso for Passover, or should I? Your mom's really excited, so we need to book them soon.

DAVID: I think I can do it. I have to run though, Amy's sitting in front of me and we're hashing out the budget for next season.

ME: Okay, SORRRRRRRY just wanted to make sure we didn't disappoint your mom, who's really looking forward to this trip.

DAVID: I know, sorry and thanks for thinking of it. Means a lot. Love you.

PERFECT. Quick and guilt inducing, but balanced out by the fact that I have a (totally genuine) love and concern for his mom's happiness. But when there are no logistics to discuss, my cover stories get a little less focused:

DAVID [picks up]: Hey, everything okay?

ME: Why wouldn't everything be okay?

DAVID: Because you just called.

ME: Yeah . . . um . . .

DAVID: What's up, I have the editors all here . . .

ME: I'm busy, too, you know. Reminder, I work almost full-time and when I'm not HEALTHILY contributing to this family in a financial sense, I'm tending to the emotional gardens of our children!!

DAVID: I know you are and I thank you for that every day. Thank you.

ME: You're welcome.

Beat.

DAVID: Soooo . . . is that it??

ME: No, as a matter of fact, I'm wondering . . .

DAVID: Yeah???

ME: Hi.

DAVID: YES??

ME: Um. I have a funny story.

DAVID: No, you don't.

ME: Yes, I do and it's pertinent.

DAVID: To what?

ME: You. Us!

DAVID: Okay, think of one really quick—

ME: I don't need to think of one, *David* [Alexis from *Schitt's Creek* voice], because I know what it is. *(Scanning my brain for any story at all to recount.)* So . . . um . . . Laura was running to print something at Kinko's—

DAVID: Why doesn't she have a printer?

ME: Not everyone has that luxury, David.

DAVID: Okay, and what?

ME: And a woman accidentally hit her in the head with a bag of bagels.

DAVID: Jesus. Is she okay?

ME: Yeah. Then she said something so funny about the universe. It was like, the universe doesn't want good things for me. Or . . .

DAVID: That's really . . . sad. Can we talk later? The editors just left because I was on the phone for so long and now the entire writers' room is waiting for me.

ME: Well, I'd love to talk later but I'M GOING TO BE WITH OUR CHILDREN ALL AFTERNOON, SO, SORRY THAT I WANTED TO SAY HI BEFORE I GET ENGULFED IN THEIR SEA OF NEEDS.

DAVID: Okay, sorry, hi. I love you.

ME: Do you?

DAVID: Yes. Okay, talk soon.

It's at these impasses when it becomes clear to me that the only way to keep him on the horn is to launch into one of my rants. It's easy, though, because my favorite one immediately comes to mind.

> **ME:** Wait, important question. For REAL. For real, for real. Super quick. I'm super stuffed up and I *(lying)* think I'm getting sick and *(lowering my voice, gravely)* I have to ask you something.
>
> **DAVID:** Okay, hold on, I'm stepping out. What's up?
>
> **ME:** How do you get the Afrin bottle open?
>
> **DAVID:** You had nothing to ask me when you called, did you? Not one thing. And you aren't sick, I can tell, but you *are* addicted to Afrin.
>
> **ME:** I agree I may have an . . . issue with it, in that I have come to depend on it or my nose cavities seem entirely closed, but I'm not ready to tackle that issue yet. What I AM ready to tackle is how to get that fucking childproof top off. I tried bludgeoning it with a wrench and still can't get it open. And I'm not the only one! Google "Can't open Afrin" and you'll find a community of like-minded individuals out there who are every bit as enraged!!!! For starters, they're stuffed up as helllll. And now, they can't get a simple red top

off. I have a bachelor's degree in drama with a partial minor in women's studies and I can't get a top off???? The directions say "turn over the bottle, push down on the tip and lightly turn the top to open." Well, that's bullshit. My greatest dream?? My FONDEST wish??? Is to watch the CEO of Bayer (parent company to Afrin) sit in an empty room with only his bare paws and see if he can open that bottle. I want to see the blood drain from his bloated red face, entitled white male alcoholic that he no doubt is, as he realizes he's NEVER going to be able to remove it. NEVER. I want to see him become so infuriated he goes insane and after trying to smash the top off with the metal chair he was sitting in in an effort to dislodge it, he finally throws the chair at the three-way glass I'm watching him through, and then has to be tranquilized and eventually locked up like Blanche DuBois at the end of *Streetcar*.

DAVID: Okay . . .

ME: I bet he's never even opened one bottle. Never even fucking bothered to try it himself, has the chemists or his assistants open it for him so he doesn't even know the fatal flaw of his otherwise brilliant product.

DAVID: I mean, I don't think the CEO invented it . . .

ME: But he's responsible. And he needs to know. YOU CANNOT FUCKING OPEN IT!!!!! No—you know what I want more than the three-way-glass thing?

DAVID: It's called two-way glass.

ME: I want him to go on that show *Undercover Boss*
and get on the front lines, away from all the fat
cats and his corner office overlooking downtown
Philly or wherever, and be forced to work among
his hardworking employees who toil away every day
making his precious Afrin. Or better yet—make him
sit in a call center as part of the Customer Service
Team receiving call after call after call of people
telling him straight up, it won't open.

DAVID: I don't know that Afrin has a team of people
working in its call center. Or even a call center.

ME: And all that CEO will be able to do is sit there
helplessly because, as the cute gal working next to him
says, "We have nothing to tell them. There's no way to
get it open."

DAVID: I've gotten it open for you several times. I mean
I think they just don't want kids to be able to—

ME: And then by the end of the show he'll break down
and promote an underling, that gal, and thank her in
front of everybody for actually being HONEST. And
right then and there he announces a recall will be
taking place of all tops—effective immediately—and
the people who rely on it and need it, because WHEN
YOU NEED IT YOU NEED IT, will never again have
to suffer congestion while a bottle sits next to them,

unopened. It's humiliating, and frankly? It's just
wrong.

DAVID: Case, I've heard all of this before and I HAVE
to go.

ME: SO DO I! I work full-time-ish because I can't work
full-full-time due to your schedule and choices while
you get to skip off to work, not a care in the world,
free to follow your dreams full throttle, whereas, when
I go to work I'm preoccupied with the mental load of
where the kids are, what needs to be done, who needs
to be picked up, who needs to go where, etcetera.

DAVID: And I really appreciate that. I tell you all
the time what an amazing mom you are and how
astounded and inspired I am by all you do and
accomplish and how you're also the funniest person I
know. And I gotta say, when we divided up the jobs of
the household on that napkin I took on a lot more—

ME: Not enough! You tried to say "Social Lubricant"
was one of your jobs. That's not a job, that's a
personality trait. And everyone knows I'm way more
social than you. You haven't made a plan or hung
out with one friend since we got married, unless it
was planned by me. What would my mother say?
She fought on the front lines for the Equal Rights
Amendment, literally leading the charge to add "And
women" to the Constitution. But it didn't pass in
Congress and it hasn't passed in our house.

DAVID: Okay, that's a much larger conversation, but I do think I do more than you give me credit for and truly, I'm not even wanting or needing credit, I just think—

ME: I realllllly don't want to get into all this right now. I just want to get my Afrin open.

DAVID: I get the Afrin bottles open! That's one thing I definitely do.

(Pause. He's got me there.)

DAVID: Okay, I HAVE TO GO. But in case you do get it open, I want to remind you that Dr. Cohen forbade you to use it again. She's told you multiple times it's highly addictive. Just like Chapstick, it's designed to make you need it!

Then it hit me. I was doing to David what Afrin was doing to me. Creating a dependency. All I needed to do now was make my top harder to get off. To make him want it all the more.

(Shifting my tone. I'm all-business now. Brusque.)

ME: I gotta run.

(Shifting his tone. Thrown by my sudden dismissiveness.)

DAVID: Where are you going?

ME: Here and there. Bye, seriously, I'm late.

DAVID: Oh. Okay. I mean one second ago you had all the time in the world to talk. And now—

ME: Yeah but that was one second ago. Now we're in this second. Now this one.

DAVID: K. Love you. Miss you. See you at—

I don't hear the rest because I've hung up.

I get in the car, proud of how I've conducted and comported myself.

I start driving. Call a few pals. No one picks up. Try a podcast. Boring. Sit with my own thoughts. No thanks!

I can't help myself . . .

ME: Okay, ONE more thing.

DAVID: Yes????!!

(Pause.)

ME: What's up?

He hangs up and we're back to one. Unequal balance restored. I just love him.

Grandpa's Pretty Girl

Just as my grandfather's funeral was about to start, an elderly man in jean shorts approached me, to my befuddlement. The jean shorts were not unusual for a Pensacola, Florida, funeral. I was touched he had dressed up; I just didn't recognize him. He was breathless, and clutching a cassette tape.

"I want to sing. I have to sing," he said, peering up at me with watery eyes.

Hmmm. I was producing this funeral. The programs I'd had made at Kinko's were hot off the presses, and the detailed plan for my beloved grandpa Red's send-off did not include last-minute additions. The bill was quite full. Of me. I would be opening with "Softly and Tenderly," an old Baptist hymn my grandfather loved, and closing with "In the Garden," another favorite. In between, I'd be treating honored guests to "Farther Along" and "Amazing Grace." When I wasn't singing, I'd be speaking, though I'd graciously allowed a couple others to pipe in: his son and my brother, *if* they kept it brief. Was I singing too many songs? Many said as much, but I wasn't gonna take that worry on.

I'd learned to sing from my grandfather. He had a beautiful, quivering southern twang and could harmonize with any melody. After my grandma died, I'd often find him sitting in "his chair" singing snatches of lyrics aloud to himself—his favorite lines from Hank Williams's "I'm So Lonesome I Could Cry" or Willie Nelson's "Hello Walls" or any Johnny Cash song. As far as I was concerned, Grandpa Red *was* Johnny Cash: a gorgeous, tall GENTLEman. The phrase "They don't make 'em like that anymore" comes to mind. There wasn't ONE time in all the hundreds of occasions on which I called him that he didn't answer the phone by saying, "Is this Grandpa's pretty girl?"

Marion "Red" Higdon (so nicknamed for his red hair) was such a fiercely intelligent, magnetic guy that you never would've known that his family tree consisted mostly of double first cousins. A World War II vet, he was a proud member of a truly special group of navy enlisted pilots better known as the Silver Eagles. He'd been a Republican all his life until the very end, when he told me, "Sugar, I can't stand George W. Bush, he's gonna ruin this damn country," and cast a ballot for Al Gore. Not too many southern men in their mid-eighties change their minds or their politics. Maybe it had something to do with the fact that he had raised a feminist daughter and a gay son, my beloved uncle Alan, who died of AIDS in the late 80s. But whatever the reason, he had softened and changed over the years, which soooo few people do.

He may or may not have had a drinking problem in the way that everyone in the "greatest generation" seemed to have. But nobody cared, because when he drank he only got funnier and his sparkling blue eyes only got kinder. Every time I visited, when the clock ticked 5:00 P.M., he'd put down his horse racing forms, take off his glasses, give me a wink, and say, "Fix Grandpa a smile." Age nine, I'd hand him his Johnnie Walker on the rocks and pad into the kitchen to get *my* smile: the candy he had bought for me in BULK from the grocery store on the naval base because one time I'd said I liked them. Anyone who says food isn't love has never sat on wall-to-wall carpeting eating peanut butter M&M's, leaning up against their grandpa's leather chair, listening to the ice cubes in his drink clink while they watch TV in companionable silence.

Grandpa Red hated it when anyone would go to any trouble for him. Despite this, our family planned a big party for his eighty-sixth birthday at his nursing home, Coldwater Creek (just up from the Winn-Dixie on Bayou Boulevard), and everyone flew in from all over. My dear aunt Sharon and I were going over the party details with him two days prior to it when he corrected me. "Sugar, it's not gonna be my birthday party, it's gonna be my funeral."

He died that night.

And so here we were, two days later, and a man I did

not know was begging to sing at his funeral. I asked him if he knew my grandpa from The Creek.

He nodded, looking as distressed as I felt. "Your grandpa loved my singing," he said.

I put my hand on his shoulder. "Sir, if my grandpa Red loved your singing, then I have a spot for you, indeed. We would be honored if you would close us out."

He smiled bashfully, revealing his lack of teeth, and it occurred to me that he might have been intimidated because he had seen ME perform. Not from TV or film, but from The Creek.

In the previous two years, I'd made quite a name for myself there. I'd arranged with the staff to do mini-concerts in the sanctuary/craft room, and my performances ran the gamut. Once, I treated residents to all the classics from the Great American Songbook; on another occasion, I reenacted *The Sound of Music* and played all the parts. NOT EASY, sweeties. After my last appearance, I'd asked my grandpa if everyone was impressed that his granddaughter came all the way from New York City (well, Bay Ridge, Brooklyn) to sing for them.

"Not really, sugar. Melvin's granddaughter is playing Maria in *The Sound of Music* on Broadway right now, and she often flies here on Monday mornings between shows. She's really something."

What those elders at The Creek didn't know is that I'd come close to many, MANY parts I would not get. But I'd come close! A few years earlier, Christopher Guest, my mom's and my all-time favorite director, was casting a small part in his upcoming mockumentary, *For Your Consideration,* and I had an appointment to audition. My body felt like it was exiting the atmosphere. I'd punctured the solar system. I WAS A STAR!!!!!!!!!!!!! I called my mom FRANTICALLY and we screamed and screamed. Our favorite director! This was meant to be! The part called for "a brunette"!!! My mom had never been so excited. I had quite literally just moved to LA, but I'd been at this for a few years and . . . nothing. This was IT.

That phone call was the last time I spoke to her. The next morning my dad called to tell me she had passed away in the night of a heart attack. I completely forgot about the audition. I was without the woman I loved most in the world, and on top of that, I had my first funeral to produce.

For my mom's service, I booked a lineup that would melt hearts and blow minds. The flip side of this is that it was three and a half hours long. That is no exaggeration. I became more and more racked with anxiety over the length with each passing minute. It had spiraled out of control. I worried people were upset it wasn't over. About two hours and forty minutes in, I whispered to my dad, "It's running too long! What do we do???!"

He didn't even look away from the speaker. Quietly and peacefully, Dad said something that I will never forget. "Casey. If, at the end of this, we turn around and there isn't a soul in the seats, I'm okay with that. This is for us."

And it was. My father would later bring the DVD copy

of the funeral on a whistle-stop tour around the country in his Acura, hitting up friends of my mom from over the years who hadn't been able to make it to the main event. He set up photos of her on an easel he traveled with and would fast-forward to "highlights." It looked pretty good—since my dad makes political commercials for a living, he was able to film it with three cameras. He spent a lot of time editing it and capturing everyone's best angles, and even brought me in for ADR on my eulogy. ADR is when you rerecord any parts where the sound may have dropped out during the original recording. Something only ever done for movies and television shows. Not funeral speeches. He finally got me in the sound booth over Christmas, and as I redid my "lines," he yelled from behind the glass, "That's great, Case, but you had more emotion on the day. Let's take it back."

It was all so surreal. But rerecording my choked sobs after the fact was nothing compared to the horror show the day of, at the open-casket viewing for my mom. Upon seeing and saying goodbye to my mom, a Dolly Parton–esque woman bounded up to me. "Excuse me, baby girl, was it your mama that passed? I did her makeup, you know . . . today . . . and I was wuhnderin', do you happen to know if she had an eye lift?" She had. "Could you possibly give me the name of the doctor, because she looks so darn good!" Processing this interaction in the hearse en route to the church for the service, I concluded that my mother had been paid a high compliment and filed the encounter under: success.

I couldn't say the same about the man seated in between my brother and me in the hearse. He was my dad's first cousin, a man *everyone* called Jimmy Jet. He was a commercial airline pilot who'd claimed to have seen "them" lingering just above cruising altitude. "Them" being . . . aliens. He's a very nice guy who also happens to believe steadfastly and wholeheartedly in aliens. So! It was very sweet of him to fly to Virginia for the funeral even though the fact that he jumped into the hearse with my dad and brother and me after the viewing was a bold move. As we headed for our church, Jimmy started whistling, as though he had not a care in the world. Then, no doubt sensing that he'd struck the wrong tone, he turned to my dad to address him, gravely.

"You know, Paul. Masala has some more updates for you." Masala, Jimmy Jet's spiritual leader, lived in the D.C. area, so Jimmy was "killing two birds with one stone" on this trip.

Periodically he'd call my parents in the middle of the night and whisper, "Hey Kath, how are you, Masala says the world is ending on May twenty-second."

"Thanks for the call, Jimmy!" my mom would say brightly and go back to sleep.

Now, apparently, Masala had some new dates, since the old ones seemed not to have been so accurate, as here we were. (Well, here some of us were.) "Paul, Masala says we need to look out in February. The creatures are—"

My dad cut him off with another line I'll never forget, because my dad has never cut off a soul in his life.

"Jimmy," he said, "we're thinking about Kathy right now. Not aliens." Poetry.

When we arrived for the funeral, we were presented with a beautiful canvas cloth to drape over the coffin, made by the kids at the preschool where my mom worked, decorated with their colorful handprints. This gift was so simple and so beautiful and so special to us that later that month, my dad had the cloth cut into three pieces and framed, then gifted a third to my brother and me for Christmas. We cherished these scraps of fabric like lifelines. "THIS WILL NEVER NOT BE OVER MY MANTEL!!!" I vowed. But because my shithole of an apartment didn't have a mantel, I propped it up against a wall and slept on the floor, next to it. For a year. As you do.

The days that followed my mom's death were what you would call strange for my dad. He got a PERM after finding a twenty-dollar bill on the ground. The same way I might bring a picture of Kate Hudson to my hairdresser and ask for "The Kate," he brought the rumpled bill and asked for the Andrew. "Jackson me!" he told Terry, his hairdresser. She told me later she didn't want to, but he was so adamant. She Jacksoned him all right. It did oddly suit him. He started getting spray tans that never seemed to reach all the way up to his hairline, and tweeting. Tweeting might have been a good outlet for his musings, but unfortunately, he started tweeting messages he'd intended to text: "Be there in five minutes," "How are you," "Call me," and lots of pocket missives like "Ppppxppp." (Follow him @powilson. Questlove does!)

He then paid over a thousand dollars for a seven-foot (!) portrait of himself, which he gave to me and my husband because "since mom died everyone only has photos of her around!"

A lot happened, see photo evidence.

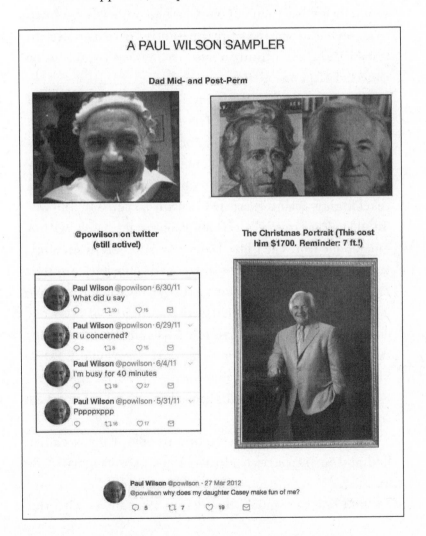

A PAUL WILSON SAMPLER

Dad Mid- and Post-Perm

@powilson on twitter (still active!)

The Christmas Portrait (This cost him $1700. Reminder: 7 ft.!)

Paul Wilson @powilson · 6/30/11
What did u say

Paul Wilson @powilson · 6/29/11
R u concerned?

Paul Wilson @powilson · 6/4/11
I'm busy for 40 minutes

Paul Wilson @powilson · 5/31/11
Ppppxppp

Paul Wilson @powilson · 27 Mar 2012
@powilson why does my daughter Casey make fun of me?

Not much was happening on my end in Los Angeles. June and I had started writing on an animated CBS show, and in an astonishingly misguided move, both of us asked for raises on DAY ONE. We had worked hard that first part of that first day! That raise was denied. We would lie for each other about where we were when we had to go on auditions and were constantly "getting prescriptions filled" and "fixing a flat tire." The show would be canceled after one airing.

Then one day, while pretending to write, I received a call about that Christopher Guest movie I was supposed to audition for a year before. *For Your Consideration* was totally finished, but Christopher (Mr. Guest?) had decided to add a final scene in which Catherine O'Hara is teaching an acting class. Did I want to come in and audition for the role of a girl auditioning for a role with a monologue from the Bette Davis movie *Jezebel*? I sure did. It was clearly fate that this movie had come back around. How fitting would it be for me to get my very first part in *this* movie. A movie that was the subject of my final call with my mom. She had never seen me get anything, really, and I felt like if I got this part, she would KNOW. She could even be responsible for it!

I bawled my eyes out in the parking lot after I bombed the audition.

But the next day, pretending to edit, I got a call. I had gotten the part. And then I got another part. And another.

And one day, much much later, the canvas with the

children's handprints was moved to my younger son Henry's bedroom. And my dad got remarried and moved his to the basement. Beyond photos of her, the only remaining physical reminder of my mom is when we hang her stocking at Christmas, as though she's receiving stocking stuffers somewhere in the sky. I hope she is.

And I hope that way, way up there in the great beyond, Grandpa Red isn't upset that I allowed someone I found out he had never met close out his funeral. An elderly stranger who would rap a song, off beat, about Jesus over a cassette tape of children's backup vocals that stopped midperformance because the ribbon had snarled from overuse. That did not stop him from finishing a cappella, though.

He was our closer. We all sat there, horrified.

It is my great hope I don't have to produce any more funerals for a long, long while.

It Doesn't Do

My family has spent nearly every Thanksgiving with my parents' college friends the Brennans. Occasionally we would host it at my parents' house and my mom would cook, leading one boyfriend to remark, "I appreciate how much your mom has done for women's rights, but this food is the by-product." I couldn't disagree. So after many dry turkeys and green bean casseroles, my parents threw in the towel, and now we do it exclusively at the Brennans' in Maryland.

My brother formed lifelong best friendships with each of their four kids and dated two of them, but because I was the oldest, I regarded them like additional little siblings and bossed them around relentlessly. When she was four, I cut Maddie Brennan's bangs with a pair of gardening shears.

Steve Brennan is my dad's best friend and the person my father prioritizes above everyone else on Earth. They have had breakfast together every Saturday for thirty years, and during the pandemic they've shared this ritual over Zoom. Lorraine Brennan is the gentlest woman, who never has an unkind word to say about anyone. The opposite of my mom, though the two of them were incredibly close friends.

Thanksgiving dinner plays out the same way every year. Lorraine cooks all day for all fifteen of us and then everyone pitches in to clean up but me. Having kids has really solidified my role as the person who does absolutely nothing to prepare the meal or pick up after it. The kids nap till five! I have to get the kids to bed!

The cast of characters rarely changes. The Brennans, Fletcher and me, and whoever we're dating or are married to, my dad and mom, later my dad and one of his girlfriends, eventually my dad and my wonderful stepmom, Marjorie, Lorraine's mother, her sister, Judy, and Judy's husband and their son. Things play out pretty much the same every year. After drinks Lorraine calls us all to the table and we take our seats. If my dad isn't seated near the younger set he'll mouth to Fletcher and me, "What about Daddy?" mournfully, and if we ignore him he'll whimper like a dog louder and louder until someone makes a spot for him. He hates being left out.

Two years ago, the conversation turned to politics when someone brought up the #MeToo movement. "Someone" was most likely my dad, who had and has a lurid fascination with who will be outed next. Each time a new man is accused he calls me breathlessly, like a teenage girl reporting hot goss, and says, "Guess who's going down now?!!?"

He uses this same tone when he waaaaaay too enthusiastically reports terrible news about his beloved friends:

"Jerry Richardson died! Riddled with cancer. Tip to tush. Doctors told him he had three months. Wrong. TWO. WEEKS."

"Your uncle? The one I wouldn't ever let you be alone with because I was afraid he would molest you? Donnie Jr.? Dead. It's real sad. I'm gonna help pay for the funeral."

But most of the time the information he's sharing is just wrong.

"Tom Cookler died. Fletcher's soccer coach? Awful."

One day later, a voicemail update: "Shoot. Tom's alive. Got that wrong. It was your preschool teacher who died. Murdered. By a VERY jealous ex. She was always very pretty so. . . . What was her name? Brandi. No, Brielle. Damnit. MONICA! Monica was murdered. Tom, on the other hand, couldn't be better. Joined a new indoor soccer league."

It's always a roller coaster. My brother is the most horrified by this tendency of my dad's, and calls him out when he joyfully REPEATS tragic news to us, having forgotten he shared it the second it happened. Fletcher will get really fired up, telling him, "It's almost like you're turned on by it. Extreme weather, too. You're titillated by the idea of millions of people on the verge of losing their homes."

So when the #MeToo movement came up at dinner, I knew my dad's interest would be piqued. "Anyone new gone down?" he asked the table, in case he'd missed any breaking news between grace and pie. Right off the bat,

Lorraine's elderly mother hits us with five words you don't want to hear, "So men can't flirt anymore??!" I contemplated calmly standing up and flipping Lorraine's beautifully set eight-foot table but realized that then I would have had to help with cleanup.

"I think it's been really hard on everyone." I looked up to see who was piping in next. It was Lorraine's sister, Judy. I had known her for years and never known what to make of her, but after moving to the West Coast I realized what I'd been seeing all along. A Palo Alto hippie-liberal/struggling visual artist who prided herself on her funky chunky jewelry and *New Yorker* subscription. We gave her our full attention.

"I'm just saying, the #MeToo movement's been hard on everyone. On . . . me." No one moved. Judy was about to confide in us and share a difficult incident from her past right here and right now. And my dad was here for it. He leaned so far forward he almost dropped his Kahlua and coffee.

"I just mean . . . everyone's coming out and saying they were raped or touched or fondled or ogled inappropriately or whatever and . . . well . . . what about those of us who . . . weren't?" We cocked our heads gently, struggling to follow her train of thought. "How are *we* supposed to feel that no one even wanted to do that stuff to us?"

I haven't heard that kind of deafening silence since a wealthy mom-friend encouraged the members of our Mommy and Me class to buy a seventeen-hundred-dollar earthquake kit from Goop.

Judy was staring at us, awaiting our heartfelt condolences. It was challenging. But it was Thanksgiving, so
everyone mumbled a word or two all at once. The words
tumbled out on top of one another like waves upon the
shore.

"Huh . . ."

"Yeah . . ."

"I guess I never thought of it that way . . ."

"Well . . ."

"That's really . . . something to ponder . . ."

"Did I black out?"

"WHAT IS HAPPENING?!"

"So men can't flirt anymore?"

On the drive home, had my mom been alive, she would
have 100 percent used her favorite sound bite for when
someone does something ABSOLUTELY INSANE. It's a
southern phrase her dear friend Nancy Foil's mom used
in moments like this. "It doesn't do to talk about it." And
then after a pause, "It doesn't do."

So many moments haven't "done" since she passed
that I wish to God I could tell her about. One such moment happened soon after her funeral, my first week back
in Los Angeles. I was trying to lie low and limit my inter-
actions with humans because I was in an absolute daze. I
was having trouble finishing sentences, let alone appearing the way I wanted people to perceive me at all times,
which is upbeat and normal. Normal is a label I prize
above all else. This stems from growing up with parents
who didn't care what people thought or how they were

perceived. One year, during a Christmas decorating party at our church my mom stretched out and fell asleep on a pew. "She's just tired!" I frantically told fellow parishioners as we dragged garlands over her face and body. My dad was up to stuff a normal person would never dream of. If he was late for a flight (which was always) he would routinely abandon his car in front of the airport, using their towing company as his own personal valet and the impound lot as his parking spot. "Cheaper than missing the flight!" he told us, proudly.

Hats off to them, but as their child I felt like I had to play the straight man to balance them out and keep people from writing us off. I was constantly following them with a metaphorical dustpan and broom and a panicked "nothing to see here!" look in my eyes. I was like the hot young wife in a multicam sitcom who is inexplicably married to Kevin James and can't have any fun of her own because her sole purpose is to finger wag and tamp down her "crazy husband"!

And so here I was, wandering into Joan's on Third in a fog, praying I wouldn't see anyone I knew. Joan's on Third is an upscale, trendy, glorified deli where the sun bounces relentlessly off the aluminum outdoor furniture and you sit on the sidewalk on display and wonder why you ever moved to Los Angeles.

I was in line ordering when, naturally, a comedy writer I knew, Andy Secunda, got in line behind me. Andy is a sweetheart. He once called me after seeing how little screen time I was getting on *SNL* and volunteered to send me sketches I could pass off as my own. I knew him from my Upright Citizens Brigade days back in New York, but now his sister was my agent and I hadn't seen him in a while. From his jaunty, chatty tone, I could tell he hadn't heard about my mom, and this plunged me into darkness. Bumping up against cheerful, normal people who are ditty-bopping about their days, ordering mac and cheese and Chinese chicken salads, is a jarring injury when your world has collapsed. You feel angry at them, though they have done nothing wrong, and jealous of them, from inside your private bubble of hell. I felt like there was actual glass between us as he went on, updating me on his improv show and asking me what I was working on. Burying my mother! I wanted to say.

"This and that. June and I are writing a movie . . ." He lit up, genuinely happy for me. We started talking about an exciting new project he was pitching but it was as though he was speaking in a different language. I couldn't understand a word he was saying. Because we were in fact speaking two different languages. It was clear. His life was moving forward and mine had ended.

And then. As we paid for our food and were walking outside, I remembered. A couple months ago, his sister had told me their mom was sick. This whole time he had been in the same hell as me. I cut him off midsentence and touched his shoulder, reaching out of my bubble to connect us.

"Andrew. Your mom. How is she doing?"

A taxi pulled up in front of us. "I'm so sorry, I'm late

for work. My car's in the shop so this is for me." He started getting in the car but looked back at me meaningfully. "My mom's doing great, Casey. Thank you so much for asking. She's made a complete and total turnaround. I'm so happy!"

Before I could respond, the taxi started to pull away from the curb. As it merged into traffic, Andy furiously rolled down his window and stuck his entire head out of it, shouting back to me, "Wait! Did I hear something about *your* mom?"

The taxi suddenly lurched forward, and as it sped away I yelled back, as not to be rude and leave this question unanswered, "OH, SHE'S DEAD! MY MOM'S DEAD!"

It does not do.

What Dis

I consider myself a confident person. I had an assistant when I was an assistant. I sent Oprah and Gayle King invitations to my wedding. I still suck my thumb and don't care who knows it. (Mostly. Don't tell anyone.)

But every part of motherhood throws me for a loop. Prepregnancy I am told I have negative eggs to work with. My actual pregnancy is lovingly labeled "geriatric and obese." And once my son is finally in my arms, the reality that I'm raising a human shakes me like a rattle. The ground beneath me gives way. And not just because I have the kind of crippling postpartum depression that results in my casually asking other moms, "When you're driving do you feel like all the cars around you are about to explode and engulf your kids in flames?"

While normally I find indecision to be a devastating character flaw, I have become a nervous wreck: Am I doing this right? Am I doing *that* right? Why won't he latch? Is my sadness affecting him? Is the fact that I listened to Kanye West's "Only One," a song about his late mother looking down on him and his new baby daughter, over and over while wailing going to affect him long-term? Why did I pick a preschool he hated? Why did I accidentally lock my keys in a 107-degree car with him *in* it? (A memory he brings up often—most likely his first—is the story of when "the men went boom boom boom with a hammer on the front window and Mommy was crying.") So much crying. So much doubt. Peppered with moments of soaring elation and gratitude that the universe would deliver me such a perfect, dear, empathetic, funny, creative, curious, old soul.

ANYTHING THAT GOES wrong is my fault, and anything that goes right (quite a bit, actually) is in spite of me.

And even things that are clearly out of my control— like when a psychic tells me our nanny has put a curse on my son in order to make him think she is his mom—feel like my failure. And the fact that I don't even have time until the next day to go to a fabric store to purchase the red string that I'm supposed to tie on his left hand in order to break the spell is clearly ON ME.

I examine my every moment with him for flaws. It always feels like I'm hovering outside my body, watching and judging my performance. Initially I think this is because of the moment of parenting we're in now, in which women are meant to feel grateful that feminism has granted us the opportunities to work full-time and be simultaneously ferociously dedicated to our children in a way generations of parents before us have never been. You can have it all if you're cool with working two full-time shifts (if you're lucky) in and out of the home and driving yourself crazy with guilt and misery about the things you AREN'T doing. All in the name of being a "good mom."

That's all, as my therapist would say, "in the marinade," but it doesn't help that I also feel deep, deep within myself that something is actually really wrong. Wrong with my son. At two years old he seems . . . depressed. Melancholy. I often find him lying on the ground when I enter a room, gazing at the ceiling with such a sense of longing it makes my heart physically hurt. His teacher reports that while the other kids are playing he often lies on the couch and just watches, looking as though he hasn't slept in days. He sleeps fourteen hours a day, though. Sometimes sixteen. He has tantrums that seem intense and unending even for a two-year-old, and his reactions to transitions are so outsize they leave us struggling to console him. Playdates are tense because I am desperate for him to connect and play and have *fun* with other kids. But he usually asks to leave as soon as we get there or doesn't engage whatsoever, and I drive home in tears, demoralized.

In the car after one such afternoon I ask him what he wants to be when he grows up and he replies: "A stranger. A stranger who sits alone in a movie theater eating popcorn and no one talks to them." Huh. Now, obviously this is my dream career as well, but for a two-year-old it implies something is off. I just don't know what.

On a week-long vacation with my best friend, Amanda, and her sister, who have *six* boys between them, I watch with envy as the other kids play their hearts out, wrestling and clobbering each other in the pool, doing cannonballs directly onto each other's heads. At this exact moment my son, who sits watching from a pool chair, turns to my friend and me and says earnestly, "Beautiful breeze in the trees."

Amanda, my best friend since third grade, is now a child psychologist, and two weeks after our vacation, she calls and in a genuinely loving way asks if she can ask me something hard. "Case, do you think maybe he's autistic?" We get him tested. He isn't.

He's just sad, he tells me. Just sad. Sad because Nicholas pushed him at the preschool he hates. Because his tummy hurts. Because he feels angry. We read our favorite book, *When Sophie Gets Angry—Really, Really Angry . . .*, about a girl who gets so mad at her little sister she runs away from home into the woods. Then she climbs a tree and looks out at all below her, the sky and the trees and the ocean, and the narrator says, "The wide world comforts her. And Sophie isn't angry anymore."

My little guy (like me) is angry a lot. I've jokingly told a few moms at his school that living with him is like living with an abusive alcoholic. I'm terrified of him! They don't seem to find this funny, and again, I think: *I'm having a different experience than most moms are having.* And then I'm angry again.

And I hate myself for the excuses my husband and I make to each other and others for his behavior and his moods. He didn't get a good night's sleep, his blood sugar's low, he woke up on the wrong side of the bed, he's a little shy, he's a loner, he's an indoor cat!

But what really bothers me is not that this is his temperament—because it really would be fine if that's the case—but more that I'm not sure this is actually his temperament. Because a few times a day, usually when he's alone with my husband and me, we see bursts of such life force and wholehearted engagement and imagination it's staggering. He yells, "Look, Mama!" at everything he does, so excited to share and connect over every new discovery, his face shining with joy. And he is a budding comedian. Doing pratfalls and copying our cadences for a laugh. And in these spirited moments he asks us a question—the same question—over and over and over and over regarding every.single.thing his big blue eyes rest upon.

What dis?

Lamp.

What dis?

Book.

What dis?

Prius.

What dis?

Ambien.

What dis?

90 Day Fiancé.

What dis?

McDonald's.

He switches it up only once, when he lays his eyes on Jeff Goldblum in a Parent-and-Me class and says, quite loudly, with some amount of disdain, "*Who* dis???"

We are left wondering which version of our child is his true self. And I am left wondering how I have somehow managed to dim his bright light. Soon he is three, and the excuses I have been using to assuage my worry aren't working as well.

We seek out occupational therapy, which we're lucky enough to be able to afford, and he is diagnosed with sensory processing issues and delayed fine and gross motor skills. And "he can't jump," they tell us. "Well, white men can't . . ." I offer to lighten the mood. But inside I'm reeling. How had I not noticed he couldn't jump! He starts therapy, and for a period of time this feels like the solution.

Until he fractures his leg from a fall that couldn't even be described as a fall. (He was playing with a Matchbox car from a crouched position! It was more of a tip over.) But it has him in so much pain he screams for days whenever we even LOOK at him. This beautifully coincides with a trip to the East Coast to visit my dad and step-mom, where we have to carry him everywhere. David and I both immediately throw out our backs because we are old parents and then none of us can walk, including our infant son, Bear.

Then one spring morning, while we are speeding down the HIGHWAY after a preschool glamping trip, I happen to turn around to check on him and find him lifeless in his car seat. We have no idea what's happened and I can't find a pulse. My husband maneuvers us across four lanes of traffic in under a minute while I scream to the 911 dispatcher and try to remember how to administer CPR (another failure, not learning it well enough in my baby class). The operator asks me where we are but I have no idea. I don't even have a town to give her. She tells me she can't send an ambulance until she gets an address. We look around frantically. We are now off the exit and in a subdivision where everything looks the same and we don't see any numbers. We've also come to a complete stop at a red light and are boxed in by the cars behind us. My husband makes the inspired executive decision to back up and (lightly) hit the car behind us so that we have room to hop the curb and we begin to drive on the side-walk. We finally see an address. I yell it to the operator and my phone promptly dies. We turn off the engine and drag him out of the car to try and revive him. Both of us know something you never want to know: that this is it. We are losing him. In seconds we hear the ambulance and they load him and me into the back. I have never seen or felt such sorrow as the look on my husband's face when they tell him, "Sir, you are going to have to move your car and meet us at the hospital." David hands me Max's blanket and they shut the doors and we are off. As the paramedics work on Max, I hold his little pale hand. I start singing "You Are My Sunshine" and as I get to the end and the ambulance pulls up to the emergency room, Max suddenly moves his fingers and brushes them against my nails. I have a red gel manicure because he loves when I get my nails done red and the feel of the gels. I exhale. He is with us. Mercifully, he is okay. It was a febrile seizure, they tell us, which are apparently common for kids under six but one of the most terrifying yet benign things a parent can see. The doctor explained what we had witnessed was "just his brain resetting." Just that.

But because the seizure is followed by a rapid weight loss, we become intensely worried. "All toddlers are picky eaters!" friends tell us. The words "failure to thrive" leap to my mind. Why can't I get him to eat? I beat myself up mercilessly. "If you hadn't been so focused on your career, you would have learned to cook things beyond fish sticks and buttered pasta. You order in too much, of course he doesn't want to eat. You Postmates too much, you entitled little lazy! You once tried to Postmates a Plan B pill." (This is true. Postmates responded gracefully, "Order has been canceled.")

Our doctor confirms that yes, kids are not supposed to lose weight. Something is indeed wrong. Now he has all but stopped eating. The doctor orders blood tests. We wait.

My husband and I are going through this process together but separately. We have very different viewpoints. The main difference is my husband is optimistically convinced we just need to figure out what's going on and then we can fix it soon. Done and done. At no point does he look inward and blame himself in the *slightest*. Why would he? This is clearly no fault of ours; we are attentive, loving parents who are doing our best. Besides, he says, "I was shy growing up, and by all reports, you were a monster, so why did we think our son would be any different?"

I maintain that the blood tests will reveal the situation is absolutely dire and that it's my fault. That the thing that's going to need fixing is me. It would almost be a relief to wave a white flag of surrender and admit defeat. I am a bad mom and now everyone will be able to see what I've always known and felt. My fault, my fault, my fault.

This core belief deeply impacted my first years of mothering. My fear of inadequacy and insecurity in the face of challenges was surely felt by my son. It's like a snake eating its tail. Sometimes it felt like there was glass between us. Where my husband had a delightful, easy relationship with my son, he and I felt . . . off. Paradoxically, we also felt so close it was as though we were fused into one. It was as if I couldn't find him even though he was right in front of me.

But hadn't I been told this might be the case? When I

was pregnant with him, my friend got me a gift certificate for a session with a baby psychic, who was not a baby but rather a psychic *for* babies. He was a rode-hard-and-put-up-wet-sounding guy from Long Island who explained he would be making contact with my son in "the middle plane," while we talked on the *phone*. After locating him, he told me my son would be interested in space and dinosaurs and sports and then he added, casually, that his connection with me would "go in and out." Not really what an expecting mom wants to hear. I was thrown but plunged ahead and asked an even more potentially devastating question, which was if my son and mom, who had passed years before, were possibly in contact in this . . . middle plane. "They sure are!" he said brightly. Well, that was good news. "But they don't really hang out that much." That was hard to hear, but as my husband said later, "Not everybody likes each other."

We finally get a call from our doctor with the results of Max's blood tests. He tells us Max has celiac disease. It's a shock. Followed by a wave of unimaginable relief. Celiac disease, we learn as we frantically google, is a genetic, autoimmune disease in which eating gluten, even a particle of it, triggers an immune response in your small intestine, preventing it from absorbing nutrients. I scan past the many stomach-related symptoms and see "poor bone density, seizures, motor skill delays, learning disabilities, intense fatigue, irritability, depression, failure to thrive."

Our doctor (bless him and keep him) happens to have

done his residency under a renowned pediatric celiac specialist who quite literally wrote the book *Celiac for Dummies*. Who better to be our doctor?? After a long wait we get in with her and she holds my hand and says, "So tell me. Tell me everything." And I do. I take her through it all, and she nods the whole time. "The bad news is he has celiac. Which there is no cure for but is entirely managed with the removal of gluten." (Which, of course, isn't that bad at all.) She continues, "The good news is *absolutely everything* you're describing can be placed under the umbrella of celiac. It's textbook. And he has the highest numbers I've ever seen." (Finally, he was ahead at something!) "Give it six months without gluten," she tells us, "and I mean not one particle of a particle on a pan or in a toaster or on a cutting board, and you will see a different child."

As God is my witness, in six months, almost to the day, his truer self emerges. His essence is the very same. But he is now an outwardly thriving, happy five-year-old who is exploding with creativity and bursting with life. And still asking, "What dis?" and "Who dat?" all the livelong day.

Now, I don't mean to make this about me, but it wasn't about me!!! It had nothing to do with my failure as a mother. And that's something I've had to reckon with. Why was I so hard on myself? Why are we mothers so hard on ourselves? There's no concrete answer. But with each passing day as his health improves, so, too, does my mental health and sense of self. I'm beginning to accept that this was the start of our journey, and while it wasn't what I would have hoped, it's what happened and that's okay.

Where Max and I are now is beyond my wildest imagination. We have rebuilt. Or more-built. It's been the greatest gift I have ever received. This diagnosis and this recovery. A weight has been lifted off my heart. The other day during Zoom kindergarten (in which I am also enrolled) his teacher asks the kids to name something they like in their room that starts with the letter M. Max's hand shoots up, his eyes shining and twinkling. She calls on him—it only takes him about nine minutes for him to unmute himself—and he answers proudly, "Me. What I like in this room is me." I nearly weep.

It occurs to me then that I have never in my life said aloud (or even thought?) "I like myself"! It feels gross, somehow. Or arrogant or weak. But the part of me that resists self-love and self-compassion is the same part that assumes everything is my fault. Which makes me sad. But taking a page from my son and accessing the confidence I feel in most other realms of my life, I can look back and feel proud of the fact that following my instincts got us here. Now, can my instincts often be wrong? Sure. Like when I asked the single women at my wedding to do a flash mob dance to "Single Ladies," essentially shaming them for their singledom? (They politely declined. I'm not sure Whitney Cummings has ever fully forgiven me.) But in the case of my son, I kept asking why and searching for the answer.

And I'm proud of all moms, who attempt this debilitatingly difficult-slash-searingly magical journey called motherhood. We're all doing our best. May we believe in ourselves and have the confidence to know we are our own baby psychics.

Open-Door Policy

When my husband and I first met, he was shocked to learn I didn't lock the doors to my car or to my apartment. In Los Angeles.

I shrugged. "If people are gonna get in, they're gonna get in." He was horrified.

Safety has never been my first concern. Nor my second. Or third.

This blasé attitude likely stems from the fact that my parents placed nearly zero emphasis on it. They held firmly to the belief that people are inherently good, or they could become good with a little help, or if push came to shove they probably, mostly likely, wouldn't do anything *that* bad. It was almost as if, were they to take *any* steps to safeguard their security and that of their small children, it would mean they had given up on humanity. It would be rude for us to protect ourselves, really. It's almost like we operate with a "Take it. I dare you. It's just stuff" mentality. And it's not because we have infinite money and can replace such items willy-nilly. We do not. It's just a dangerous mix of blind optimism and the fact that we are lazy as all hellllllllll.

The front, back, and side doors to our house were rarely locked, and the door to the garage was always flung wide. This was because my dad encouraged local homeless men to come and borrow tools of any kind if the tools could help them get work. My dad is an incredibly compassionate (if boundary-less) guy. He once drove from Virginia to Baltimore with a complete stranger, a drug addict he met in the street crying about losing his kids, to attempt to represent him in his custody case. My father is not a lawyer. "He's great," my dad would say of this guy. "Now, look, sometimes he disappears on me. And sometimes he doesn't seem to recognize me, but when he's clean?? We have a lot of laughs and we pick up right where we left off."

He took a woman he met outside a Starbucks, who also suffered from a drug addiction, to the dentist many times. He paid for braces so she would have a better shot at getting a job. God love him. He didn't get me braces!

My father's efforts had mixed results. One guy tried to hot-wire his Acura, before realizing the keys were already IN the ignition and the doors were unlocked, at which point he drove off, with my dad's cell phone on the seat next to him. Leaving electronics in plain sight inside unlocked cars is a Wilson MUST. We are committed to displaying a bevy of laptops, iPads, wallets, and purses so that any criminal can truly have their pick. Looking into one of our car windows is like seeing a storefront window decorated for Christmas. What's your pleasure?

My dad called his own cell phone and the guy answered. Because my dad knew him, the guy agreed to give the phone back. "Now, Paul, I don't have the car," he added. My dad nodded sympathetically. "I understand that, Whitey." (His Christian name.) "No problem." They agreed to meet at Bread and Chocolate, a cafe in Old Town, and right beforehand my dad decided to call his friend Loren (man), a local cop. Not because my dad feared for his safety, no no no, but because he thought it would be fun to do "a sting." He met up with the car thief and chatted amiably, stalling him until Loren could sweep in and arrest him. But when my dad got home from the sting, he seemed to be filled with sadness. "They got him," he said. As though he wasn't responsible for the arrest, or as though the guy hadn't STOLEN HIS CAR. "They got him."

Our family has been pretty lucky actually, considering. This ethos soaked into my generation, and while I think and hope that my brother and I have inherited his compassionate nature, in terms of self-protection, we have become just as laissez-faire.

When I pull up to my house after a long day, the idea of taking my purse and my trash inside can feel like a bridge too far. Even my keys feel heavy. We've been taught to practice self-care. In that moment, knowing my husband is on set and I have two toddlers to face, alone, from the hours of five to whenever I can manage to get them into bed, makes me feel like I simply cannot do one more thing. Having my stuff stolen almost feels like an acceptable trade-off. Some women have the same feeling about having sex with their spouses at the end of the day: not one more thing. I actually do want to have sex with my husband, it's ferrying my things the ten feet from car to doorway that seems like a BIG ASK.

If my belongings are still in the car when I return, they are rotting. And a kid's backpack filled with the remnants of a school lunch left to die in the hot Los Angeles sun doesn't smell great. And if you think I regularly empty that little plastic bento box in a timely fashion when I DO manage to bring it inside, you're out of your mind.

Electronics, it turns out, also don't love to be left in the hundred-degree heat. Nor do the contents of a makeup bag. Or my half-drunk kombuchas. Or the Starbucks cup I peed in at a stoplight, dashing from work to pick my son up from school. (What choice had I????? If I'm even a minute late getting him, the preschool director looks at me with such disappointment I have to take to the bed when we get home.)

But I'm not a beast, I promise: I dump the urine out the window right after the fact and wipe myself with a towel or napkin or, in more desperate times, one of my kids' sweatshirts. It's just that bringing the cup inside and throwing it out is not something I can say I do every time. Some might even feel the fact that I don't throw it away and replace it with a fresh pee cup each morning is a sign I'm doing my part for the environment. EVERY LIT-TLE BIT COUNTS.

My husband says my car smells like a garbage dump and "the fact that you don't even smell it anymore is staggering." *So be it,* I think. Maybe my fingers are too tired from the scheduling, organizing, and arranging of our family's ENTIRE lives. This on top of two full-time jobs and the ferrying of children to and fro. Maybe my forearms are spent from providing him with the infrastructure that allows him to whistle off to his dream job with not a care in the world as to how the trains run. While those trains aren't running on time, they're running.

Life moves fast. Everyone's busy. Certain things must fall away. To quote the most boring former Real Housewife of all time, who somehow managed to give us the greatest line of all time while blackout drunk, slumped on the ground, and slurring, Teddi Mellencamp: "No longer in control of lifestyle."

No. Longer. In. Control. Of. Lifestyle.

My parents seemed to have perfect control over lifestyle. They didn't put it this way, but it felt almost as if they felt like it was lame to be those parents harping on safety. The only advice I recall being given by my dad was "If you get lost or in trouble, find a woman. She'll help you." It's actually great advice for a kid. "Find a woman." "Also," my dad added, "stay away from your uncle Bobby Jr." I never asked him for details on that one, but Bobby Jr.'s thin, greasy pony told me it was best to look but not touch.

My mom did repeat a phrase the teachers used at my preschool to teach us how to look both ways for cars when crossing the street: "No moving cars! Walk your bodies!" But that was about it.

What my mom *was* obsessive about, and I mean fervently, frothing-at-the-mouth obsessive, was drugs. She was our town's self-appointed McGruff the Crime Dog. She led the charge by organizing a weird secret society made up of nearly all the parents at T.C. Williams High School (of *Remember the Titans* fame). This group was underground for a while, as the premise was that parents wouldn't tell their kids about this group's existence but would disclose, without judgment, the names of any kids they found out, through *their* kids, who were doing drugs. She also had one of those beeping alarms installed on all our windows and doors (in 1997, way before this became a common feature). So anytime she heard a beep, she would bolt from bed downstairs in a see-through nightgown and smell our breath. Note, she didn't kill two birds with one stone and also use the alarm for security. No, it was just a means to a Breathalyzer. The doors remained unlocked.

Her obsessiveness was effective, I have to say. I have gone through life KNOWING that if I were to try cocaine, meth, crack, acid, ecstasy even ONCE I would be the unlucky one whose "heart would explode." She did a great job convincing me I didn't have the type of track record for greatness that would spare me from the random tricks of fate. I WOULD be the one to die. It reminded me of our favorite line from our favorite movie, *Terms of Endearment*. Shirley MacLaine says to her daughter, played by Debra Winger, with genuine compassion in her voice, "Emma. You are not special enough to overcome a bad marriage."

I followed in her footsteps when, as president of my senior class (not to brag, but I was also president of my sophomore and junior classes), I launched the Sober Prom Initiative! I got two hundred signatures before nearly drowning in Charlie Johnson's hot tub, so drunk was I. I also stupidly took photos of myself and my friends with my disposable camera drinking that night, had them developed, and later accidentally left the prints on the passenger seat of my car for all to see. (I told you I never bring stuff in!) I woke up the next morning and saw my mom had FRAMED the photos and scattered them all around our house. For the next month she would tell anyone who came inside how proud she was of my achievements and then point to a photo on the mantel of me guzzling a wine cooler in an iridescent Betsey Johnson dress. As punishments go, it was pretty good.

But beyond drugs, my mom was a little more looseygoosey.

One Sunday night she was at the preschool she ran, which butted up to the Baptist church we attended. She was in the middle of installing new cubbies for the Purple Diamonds when she heard some noises upstairs and got scared. It sounded like a couple of beer cans clanging together—then she heard footsteps. Then they stopped. Terrified, my mom did exactly what anyone would do, which is creep up the stairs alone and take a peek. She turned the corner past her office and saw one of the toddler nap cots had been pulled out of the closet and was lying haphazardly on the ground. Next to it was a rumpled blanket, along with a bag of Cheetos and many many many beer cans. Someone was SLEEPING here overnight.

"Hey Kath." She jumped and turned to find the preschool's part-time cook, Bill, sitting in a toddler chair eating dinner. A disheveled, quiet guy in his mid-fifties, Bill always wore the same clothes to work. Now she knew why. Sadly, Bill was homeless. And judging by the sheer number of beer cans, he most likely had a drinking problem. So once again my mom did what anyone would do, especially if they had a thirteen-year-old boy and a sixteen-year-old girl at home. She invited him to live with us.

No, she did not fire him. She gave him the key to our home (not that the doors were locked) and set up a bed for him in the basement, on the couch next to the Ping-Pong table. There was a bathroom and a separate entrance. Bill was free to come and go as long as he wasn't drinking, but my mom never smelled his breath when the door beeped at four in the morning.

I don't remember him being there that fall, but I don't remember him not being there, if that makes sense. It wasn't like we saw him every second but just when my boyfriend and I thought no one was home and started kissing on the couch, there he was. Just when my brother and his friends wanted to play a Ping-Pong tournament, there he was, watching expressionless from the couch. He certainly took no great pains to make himself scarce.

On many an evening, Fletcher and I would settle in for TGIF on the couch in the living room and find ourselves flanking Bill. I don't remember what his preferred programming was, but I do remember my brother yelling upstairs to my mom, "MOM!!! BILL WON'T LET ME WATCH MY SHOW!!!!" Bill was *incredibly* selfless and accommodating, however, when it came to my partying. He knew better than to interrupt the flow when my friends and I created a beer funnel out of a wrapping paper roll.

While he never said it aloud, perhaps because I never spoke to him, I could tell Bill was impressed with the strategy I employed in order to party and not get caught. I reserved it for anytime my dad was appearing on C-SPAN, which for a period was often, and when I knew my mom would be at work. The minute my dad's segment was up, our partying segment was up and my friends had to skedaddle. Bill seemed to have very little allegiance to my mom, but a modicum of allegiance to me, which was nice. However, when my mom found an empty bottle of white zin in my closet, I had no choice but to blame it on Bill. She didn't believe me, though, because she had found alongside it ANOTHER pack of photos of us drinking it. My mom said at that point what bothered her more than the alcohol was that I was dumb.

But as the song goes, you don't know what you've got

'til it's gone. Fall gave way to winter, and one morning my mom came up from the basement and said simply, "He's gone. Bill's . . . gone." He didn't show up to work at the preschool that day, either. Or the next day, or the one after. To no one's surprise, Bill had not given his two weeks' notice.

When the first light snow of the season began to blanket Northern Virginia, we found my mom looking out the window, pensively. "I hope he's all right out there," she said. "And I *really* hope he's not drinking." "OF COURSE HE'S DRINKING!!" I yelled. "OF COURSE HE IS!!" my brother yelled. My mom sighed and nodded sadly. "Yeah. He most likely is."

I thought that would be the end of him, that Bill, special snowflake that he was, had melted away.

But that night inches upon inches of snow fell and in the morning feet upon feet covered the streets. My brother and I flew out of our rooms and down the stairs. We knew we had a shot at a snow day. We ran to the TV, turned on the local news, and sprawled out on the Billless couch, clutching hands, hoping for good news. A local newscaster was interviewing stranded travelers at National Airport. Below her, the school closure ticker ran past the screen and finally we saw it: KINGS COUNTY SCHOOLS CLOSED!!!!!!! We jumped up and danced around the living room. It was the happiest moment of my young life, except for the time when T.C. Williams alum Dermot Mulroney screened *My Best Friend's Wedding* at the Shirlington Theatre and (because I was class president) I got to introduce him.

We flopped back on the couch. The anchor was gravely reporting how bad the weather was in a slightly aroused tone, saying, "Hundreds of people have no idea if, or when, they will be able to get home. Many were forced to sleep here—like this doctor!" The camera panned to . . . Bill.

There he was. He didn't light up the screen. Not everybody does. "Thanks, Lisa. Yeah, it's been tough. I'm just looking forward to getting back to Indiana." The reporter cocked her head sympathetically and added, "And your no doubt important work there." Bill just nodded, looking dazed, and then wandered off.

We sat there, stunned into silence.

"Humph," my mom managed, as though THIS was the first thing Bill had ever done to confuse or disappoint her.

We never spoke of Bill again. Life went on, and Fletcher and I eventually left for college and entered the workforce and fumbled toward self-actualization (pending). Midfumble, my mom passed away, and when I was home one year for Christmas I noticed my dad had done something very strange. He had locked the door. "How will Santa get in?" my Jewish son asked. I didn't bring it up with my dad, but I wondered if losing my mom out of the blue had rocked his sense that everything would be okay. The jig was up. One of US had been stolen!

A locked door was all well and good for my dad, but I wasn't ready to throw in the towel. (And thus, many towels were stolen out of gym lockers I never locked.) Yes, life had changed dramatically now that my mom was gone, but people were still good. And maybe, I rationalized hopefully, the worst was over. We had taken our emotional knocks and the rest would be smooth sailing.

And it was, for a bit. In the way life is good when you have a job and fall in love and friends and family are healthy for the most part. I have been extremely fortunate in this way. Deeply so.

But in the five years since I've had children, a sinking feeling of dread has begun to spread through me, growing stronger with each passing year. I've always prided myself on being an anxiety-free person. If anything, I had mild disdain for those whose anxiety ran amok. The notion that you would worry about something that had not happened seemed so pointless. Depression seemed so much deeper and more dignified.

Slowly but surely, though, anxiety has settled in and claimed me. And 2020 put me over the edge. Every sound is the beginning of a home invasion. Anytime I park, I vividly picture myself stepping out to get my sons out of their car seats and getting mowed down. And that's not the part that scares me. It's the fact that the police or EMTs might not check the backseat and the LA heat will suffocate them. I'm terrified of COVID, this lingering, oppressive, suffocating threat that can't be seen. I'm afraid of the way half the people in this country voted for hate, leaving our proverbial doors wide open.

I've tried to manage this newfound sensation in a number of strange ways. I attempted to build a janky, cheap panic room in the crawl space in my older son's room, but after a certain point, the contractor stopped writing me back (probably after I asked if it could also look "cute"). To keep the kids safe in the pool, I had a sensor installed that activates if even one ripple is made in the water. By activates, I mean it *blares* so loudly it has caused me another worry, which is that the sound will cause someone's heart to stop. And our neighbors do hear it, often, because wind causes ripples. A bumblebee grazed the surface of the water and set it off. At this point, I personally would rather drown than hear it go off again. Earthquakes are another fear: I sleep with my glasses under my pillow because I'm legally blind, and keep cigarettes and Starbursts in that earthquake bag, because in the event I need an earthquake bag I'm going to want cigarettes and Starbursts. That's the kind of planning I'm up to. All to give myself a false sense of security, a feeling that I can stave off the inevitable.

Which of course, I can't. Not even close. Because as I've gotten older, I know the truth. Not all people are good. Things have happened. Bad things. To friends. To family. To me. Things I couldn't have even conceived of.

And the thing I have feared most acutely has happened to a friend. She and her husband lost their beautiful children.

And so, I end with a pledge. I will never again leave a front door unlocked. Or drive after even one sip of alcohol. I'll bring in my purse. I'll find a woman. I'll only walk my body when there's no moving cars. Because it's actually arrogant not to. And it's the absolute *very* least I can do. To protect what matters most.

Mother's Day

Mother's Day is never a good day. You would think, after fifteen-plus years without my mom, I would be used to it. What it holds and now doesn't hold. But I'm not. Every year, simply put, the lights go out.

I become enraged at the families celebrating around me—specifically mothers and their adult daughters dressed in tights and ankle booties, drifting happily through buffet lines at brunch, heads in their phones, looking up only to smile for a family photo. I seethe with jealousy at daughters able to luxuriate in the phase of life when your mom becomes your friend. And I'm brought to my knees by the sight of a daughter handing her mom a homemade card from a grandkid. I choose to walk through these festivities (which you can't really avoid) with a "soft focus." "Soft focus" is a technique I was taught in acting class where you intentionally blur your vision so that your eyes don't settle on any one thing in particular, but rather everything becomes a beautiful blur. It's like noise-canceling headphones for your eyes. I need the softest of focus because my senses feel assaulted by such purposeful celebration, the celebration of THE MOTHER. When

THE MOTHER is gone, the day only serves to shine an unbearable spotlight on that absence.

This past year, my mother-in-law, who is extraordinarily lovely and deserves to be celebrated all day every day, sent this text to my husband and me: "I MADE US MOTHER'S DAY RESERVATIONS AT THE CLUB! DOES THAT WORK FOR EVERYONE?" I felt incensed. Not BY her, but FOR her: Why exactly is SHE being made to plan her own Mother's Day? It's a strange mantle to take up, but in the run up to and on the day I'll fight fights you couldn't imagine.

"UMMMM, WHY IS YOUR MOTHER PLANNING HER OWN GODDAMNED MOTHER'S BRUNCH???!!!!" I yelled to my husband across the house while putting my toddler's shoes on. "WHY AREN'T YOU DOING THE LEAST A HUMAN CAN DO, WHICH IS DIALING TEN GODDAMNED NUMBERS AND SAYING SEVEN GODDAMNED WORDS TO MAKE THIS DAY HAPPEN FOR HER!?! SHE DESERVES TO DO NOTHING ON THIS DAY AND YOU CAN'T GIVE HER THAT???!"

"Well, she's the only one who belongs to the club, so I quite literally cannot make the reservation," my husband told me evenly, seemingly used to the abuse he must take in the days leading up to M.D. This only infuriated me more.

"IF YOU CALLED, THEY WOULD TAKE THE RESERVATION!!! THEY WOULDN'T TURN YOU AWAY!!!!! THEY WOULD RECOGNIZE THE GESTURE. THE UNIVERSAL GESTURE OF A SON MAKING A RESERVA-

TION ON BEHALF OF HIS MOTHER ON HER DAY! IN FACT, I'M WILLING TO BET THEY'RE EXPECTING THAT CALL. WHAT THEY ARE NOT EXPECTING IS FOR YOUR MOTHER TO CALL!!!"

"Babe, it seems like maybe you shouldn't come this year. You seem a bit . . . upset. Which is understand—"

"OH, I WILL NOT BE JOINING!!!!" I yelled back. "I **SHAN'T** BE JOINING. I WILL NOT SIT THERE CELE-BRATING WHEN MY MOTHER CAN ONLY ATTEND BY FLYING AROUND OUR TABLE IN THE FORM OF A YELLOW BUTTERFLY. NO, I WON'T BE BRINGING A PRESENT FOR A YELLOW BUTTERFLY, BUT THANK YOU."

Since the day she died, my family and many of my mom's girlfriends believe she visits us in yellow winged form. A yellow butterfly has appeared to each of us countless times during countless pivotal life moments, and my dad and I think nothing of opening a phone call with each other by saying, "I saw Mom today. She looked good."

My husband made the executive decision as the holi-day approached to book me a massage, and on the morn-ing of, he gently suggested maybe I sit on the pool deck of the massage place, where he remembers there is a bed of roses. He didn't say it out loud, but I could tell he was hoping my mom might . . . fly by?? This was so thought-ful and sweet of him. And my spirits were temporarily lifted. But I didn't end up seeing her. My dear friend who joined me had tragically lost her mother two years after mine, and she saw a hummingbird, a symbol for her mom. But no butterfly for me.

Maybe she was . . . busy? I rationalized. Or she flew by while I was taking a sip of my spicy margarita or because I was using my soft focus to avoid the mother-daughter spa day duos scattered around the deck? Or mayyyybe she stopped by the brunch at the club, mistakenly thinking I'd be there, and then realized I was all the way across town. But I know the truth. Realistically, a butterfly couldn't get from Cheviot Hills to Los Feliz in two hours. It's just not possible. Not with traffic.

The next day my brother, Fletcher, called me with a butterfly update. This was a big deal. Fletcher's a scientifically minded, nonspiritual medical device engineer. (He'll be very annoyed I have labeled him as an "engineer," as he is VERY specific about his job title. I know this because of an email I got after I called him an engineer on my podcast. "Casey. You are my sister. Why don't you know what I do for a living? First of all, you always call it my 'job.' It's a career. Secondly, I'm not an engineer. Never have been. I got my degree in engineering but that doesn't mean I'm an engineer. Are you a 'women's studies'? I love you but I'm an entrepreneur. The CEO of two companies. I employ twenty-two people. My title is: 'Founder.'" Sheesh. I personally would stick with engineer. "Founder" sounds very made up.)

Fletcher's attachment to facts and reason is why, while I love him dearly, he's not my first call when I think I've received a "sign" of any sort or felt a "presence" of a loved one. These assertions are usually met with silence, and I've made the mistake too many times of asking why he's so quiet. Had he not heard me?? He had but, "You're not gonna wanna hear this but I think when we die that's it. Poof. You are **over**. And before you ask, no, you won't know you're over or have any consciousness that things are over because that would mean you're *not* over. No one's coming back or visiting the living or becoming a spirit on some middle plane. There is NOTHING. **You** are NOTHING." It's a lot to swallow when you're looking for a comforting word or a shoulder to cry on. He will follow up these conversations with a grim text: "THE MOST THAT HAPPENS IS OUR BODIES DECOMPOSE AND BECOME NUTRIENTS FOR THE SOIL. LOVE YA!" He also believes that if anyone has been on life support for a long time, especially anyone older, it is selfishness on the part of those keeping them alive for not pulling the plug. While he is truly the world's most fun, boisterous, big-hearted guy, it's chilling to hear that same person say over dinner, "Our planet cannot sustain keeping everyone alive endlessly because we can't say goodbye." Grim. I remind him he may have absolutely nothing to do with my power of attorney and tell my dad to triple-check that my stepmom and I are making all his decisions, promising him that in my care, I'll not only keep him alive, but I'll bring him out and prop him up *Weekend at Bernie's*–style at parties so he still feels like he's in the mix.

However, when he knows I'm really down, Fletcher

will allow that our mom MAY be coming to us as a yellow butterfly, just to pacify me. I secretly think it's to pacify himself, too, but on the whole, he's a skeptic. And sometimes I am, too. In all honesty, we've typically only seen her when we've been near flower gardens or other places butterflies usually hang out. So while I was happy to run into her at the Museum of Natural History, it was in the Butterfly Conservatory, where a sign told me there were over two hundred species of them flying around. End of the day, it still counts in my book, but it's not like I saw her in a movie theater.

But either way, I was surprised when Fletcher hit me with this. . . .

"So, I saw a yellow butterfly flying with a red one, with a smaller orange one trailing behind, and . . . hear me out. I kind of wondered if maybe Mom . . . met someone? And then . . . hear me out . . . the two of them had an orange baby?"

I paused and weighed my words carefully. I didn't want to immediately shoot down his out-of-character, improbable theory. "Look, I'd be thrilled if she met someone. But, so, are you saying her boyfriend or husband is a red butterfly? And their baby is the orange butterfly? It's hard to piece it out—but it's *certainly* food for thought."

My dad has a very different take on Mother's Day. I called him on the way back from my massage, while my children and in-laws were finishing their lovely lunch celebrating me remotely. I know better than to reach out

to my dad when I'm in the throes of darkness, but sometimes my desire for certain emotional needs to be met will
find me calling my loving father, even though I know I
won't be soothed so much as further incensed. He didn't
disappoint.

"Dad," I said. "I'm upset."

"About what???"

"Well, Mother's Day. You know it's just still such a
hard day. I wish it wasn't and I know a lot of time has
passed but it ends up being this day to reflect and I'm still
so sad she's gone—"

He cut me off. "Case, listen. This is the way of the world.
You're a mom now and it's time to just focus on that.
And if you're looking for something to feel sad about, I
met a woman in church today who told me last weekend
she and her two kids were hanging out, just tossing the
Frisbee in the backyard, when they fell into a *sinkhole*.
THAT'S bad. Imagine that! A sinkhole."

It was a lot to process. "Well, yeah, I guess . . . that is
definitely . . . bad. Very bad. Now I feel bad I even felt bad
at all. Did they get out of the sinkhole? I have to assume
if you saw her at church that they did?? I mean, look, I
know other people are going through so much worse,
it's just that today can be . . ." I scrambled and then decided to hit him back where it hurts. "You know Fletcher
thinks Mom met someone, a red butterfly, and they had
an orange butterfly baby."

My dad didn't miss a beat. "Happy for her! Gotta run
because Marjorie and I have Nats tickets."

He was right about one thing. I am a mom now and the day is also meant to celebrate me. Me, a mother. It's such a foreign concept. *How can I have kids?* I think. I'm still a child!

I'm still a nine-year-old doing Jane Fonda's workout next to my mom.

An eleven-year-old watching *Santa Barbara* with my "baby-sitter," an elderly woman named Mrs. Grimes, who smokes in bed while I sit on the floor, eating Froot Loops, hoping to grow up to be as beautiful and strong as Marcy Walker.

I'm sixteen and turning in my Latin exam blank with no name on it, hoping my teacher thinks she lost it and blames herself and, should she find it, decides to give me an A+ to cover her mistake.

I'm twenty-two and June and I are about to perform a comedy sketch at Stella By Starlight, a gala to raise money for our beloved acting school. This is a huge opportunity for us and we are as excited as we have ever been. My parents have flown in and are seated with June's parents and they are all wearing black tie. Seated in the front row are Ron Howard, Warren Beatty, Annette Bening, Mike Nichols, and Martin Scorsese. We begin singing but the mics aren't on. They never come on. Never once. No one hears one word.

I'm twenty-nine and co-*leading* a self-help retreat alongside my friend Kulap for our friends, whom we charge good money to attend. No one believes we are capable of this. (And it turned out we weren't, though

Kulap "strongly disagrees" and counters to all naysay-ers, "Have YOU been to a retreat with Jell-O shots?")

But me a *mother*?? This thought is inconceivable. That two souls depend on me and call me "Mama"??? That I am the one they will be in therapy over, the one they will pass judgment upon: Did I work too much, did I not get down on the floor and "play" enough? Did I give them enough space for their emotions? Enough space to be themselves? Did I give them *enough*???

And it is usually around Mother's Day that I feel an extraordinary pull to give them something to hold on to in the days after I am gone (God willing, gone before them). Something more tangible than a yellow butterfly.

I feel an obsessive need to give them more to cling to than what I had. And I was given quite a lot. My mom wrote me many beautiful cards over the years. Always tucked into a backpack or under covers or in a desk drawer, to be found after a visit had ended.

"My dearest Casey, it has been an honor and a privilege to see you so assuredly on the road to self-actualization."

Many are moving, some equally important musings:

"Did you see that movie *Birth* with Nicole Kidman?? What was happening with that wig?? ODD."

(But truly, what WAS happening???)

Her cards mean so much to me, I set up email accounts for each of my boys the day they were born and write of-ten. I send pictures and videos and snapshots of life and soliloquies from me about their milestones, walks we took, words they said, the many tiny, happy moments we shared. I want them to have a record, some evidence of how fiercely I loved them. It is the MOST important thing to me. To care for them—not only now, but especially after I'm gone.

And I have made my poor friends acutely aware of their marching orders concerning these accounts, should I pass. They are disturbed by the volume of emails they get from me begging them to safeguard my legacy.

SAMPLE:

Subject: When I die! ☺

Hey! Listen when I die can you log into these email accounts (see below) and both a.) print and make a book for each of my kids with everything I've sent, pictures and letters-wise, and do something concrete with the videos? I don't understand how to get them OFF the computer or if we will even want/need to when I go, but can you look into it?? Also, then get password info to them (in separate emails so they don't have to share with each other if they don't want).

Love and thanks!
Xx
Case
P.S. This is not a suicide note!

There's usually a follow-up:

One more thing and this is the main thing, can't believe I forgot to write this ☺: MAKE SURE TO STAY ON TOP OF GMAIL BECAUSE WHO KNOWS IF IT GOES BANKRUPT OR MERGES OR COLLAPSES ETC AND MY LETTERS AND PICTURES COULD BE LOST. STAY ON TOP OF THAT COMPANY!

Anything you want me to do if you die?? Happy to handle, LMK.

Xx
Casers

And sometimes another:

Last thing: you guys are so sweet to read these—haven't heard back from anyone so hoping you are getting these—but if after I die, you log in and feel like, whoa this is too many emails and photos to print and make the book, I'm sure whoever my assistant is when I die will be cool to stay on for one more week and do it for me. Just don't let too much time pass from my death so she or he is still on payroll and my death is fresh enough that they will feel badly and want to help. ONE FINAL REMINDER! GMAIL COULD END! As all good things must. Like me!

Love you guys. Xx
C Dub.

I'm so emphatic because the truth is: we never know when, as Fletcher says, it's over. I've seen it. Poof. One day you're here, one day you're not. And like anyone who's received an out-of-the-blue, life-changing phone call, you live much closer to the possibility we all fear. And I'm able to be at peace with whatever happens to me. IF I'm SURE they'll know the truth. The truth of how I loved them so.

But for now, thankfully, I'm very much alive. Alive and joyfully parenting Max and Henry Bear. A family of my own has grounded me, and with it comes a freedom and happiness I never thought I would have. My children fill me up, to the very brim. But with it comes the other side of the coin: more sadness. Sadness that my mom will never meet my husband. Or my kids. Or Fletcher's wife. Or his kids.

She will never know that in a desperate attempt to prevent us from going out to dinner, my five-year-old pleaded with my husband, "How 'bout you stay here with me while I fall asleep. You can look at jackets to buy on your phone!!!" (My husband has turned to jackets as the main tenet of his midlife crisis. He buys them ALL THE TIME and then returns them. He refers to fall as "Jacket Season." Even my son knows if anything will entice his father to stay home, it's the opportunity to scroll through images of jean jackets with faux fur collars.)

She'll never know Max saw a Hasidic man on the street, walked up to him and hugged him, and said, "Hi, Santa!"

She'll never be able to squeeze my perfect three-year-old's gorgeous cheeks. Or make fun of me that I can't decide which name of his two names, Henry Bear, to use. (And I mean I REALLY can't decide. I love both names but have concerns about each. Concerns one usually works out prebirth. I adore Henry, but it does conjure a serious banker. And Bear, I obviously love, too, but does it imply I've lost it and named my kid some weird-ass LA name like South Dakota or Story? For the first year we called him Henry and then he started calling himself Bear, so we slid on over that-a-way, but depending on who I'm with, I'll introduce him differently, eyeballing a person and guessing which one they would cotton to more. I TOLD YOU I HAVE A DESPERATE NEED TO BE LIKED!)

My mom will never know about the time at age three when Henry Bear looked around one night and said to me, quite casually but with pointed disdain, "This house is a fuuuuckin' mess." He wasn't wrong. Or about the time he looked in the mirror and smiled and said, "Why do I love looking at myself SO much?! Just, so, so much. SO MUCH." Or how when I was pushing him on the swings and said, "Look at you, you're swinging so high!" he said back casually, "Yeah, that's 'cause I'm such a great guy." He's 100 percent correct but the confidence on this kid . . .

But then again, maybe I'm right and my brother's wrong, and she does see it all. She sees Max and whatever my other son's name is playing with Fletcher's kids, Clementine and Teddy.

(If so, I hope she missed seeing my brother and me

in a very serious discussion about SWAPPING Bear and Teddy's names. This is something my brother genuinely proposed to David and me shortly after his son was born. Which gave us a THIRD option—but that felt like one too many.)

I have to believe she can. So that when all is said and done, I can finagle myself into a yellow butterfly or an orange butterfly or a hummingbird and fly above and beside them on Mother's Day and every day, loving them to pieces.

And if my friends do their jobs, my kids will always know I'm just an email away.

People Don't Know How to Act

Let's bow our heads in prayer: Dear God . . .

What would you have me do? Where would you have me go? What would you have me say, and to whom?

—Helen Schucman, *A Course in Miracles*

I say these words to myself silently, at least once a day. Sometimes more. And that's because . . . people don't know how to act. This is a phrase I got from my husband, who uses it about forty times a day. In life, he rarely gets overly frustrated or visibly angry, nor does he ever, say, sweep his most valuable possessions off the top of a dresser in one fell swoop. Because who would do that.

He will simply say, resigned, "People don't know how to act." And he's right. They DON'T.

Now, everyone has their own ideas about how one should conduct themselves as a citizen of Earth. These

opinions are my own and not the opinions of Harper-
Collins. Just my thoughts to take or leave—about how,
ideally, we should and should not behave.

Trigger Warning: You MAY see yourself reflected in
some of these examples. But then you'll likely tell yourself, "That's not me." But that's only because people don't
know how to act.

I'LL TAKE US from what I consider the smallest infractions
to the most egregious, ones that if you're guilty of, kindly
reevaluate everything.

One final note before we start: Some of these examples will seem totally innocuous. Some will contradict
one another. Some *I* am guilty of committing, frequently!
Some will make me seem like a monster for even noticing/
caring/pointing out. Some may bother me now, but if you
ask me tomorrow, I won't even remember. But in this moment in time and space, allow me to share a few things
that tweak the very core of my being.

Let's begin.

The first way in which people don't know how to
act I have just committed, and that's: too much pre-
amble. Just get to it. Please don't take up precious time
on this rock trying to figure out which day something
happened, when it's so clearly inconsequential to the
anecdote you're recounting: "So, she came over to the
house, hmm, was it Thursday? Nope it couldn't have

been Thursday, because I worked that day . . . was it . . . no, it wasn't Saturday because I was dog sitting for the O'Sullivans. . . ."

I also don't need to know who you already told this story TO. "And like I was just saying to Brenda . . ." Who is Brenda and why do I care that she already has this information?

And certainly, let's not get stumped on the *name* of the person you already told this to. "No, not Brenda, was it Deanna . . . no. Meg? Couldn't have been Meg because she's been on Bass Lake. . . ." The only exception that can be made to the preceding rules is if you are June Diane Raphael herself, the most gifted storyteller walking among us, who weaves and wields mundane details in a way that has us hanging on her every word. She can make a meal out of remembering who has already been told this story, because she'll then treat us to a sharp but true observation about said person. "It *was* Leslie! [*lowering her voice*] "Who's not one of the beautiful people, unfortunately. Anyways!"

To everyone, but especially my very beloved aunt Ann: You don't need to answer the phone with the reason you didn't answer it sooner. "Hi, I almost didn't make it in time. I heard it ring but then I couldn't find my pocketbook, and it was ringing and ringing and I yelled to Ralph, where is my *dern* pocketbook but then, thank Gorsh I found it in the couch. In the little crack between—"

ME: Well, we're here now, so . . .

ANN: I was panicking because I kept thinking, "I'm gonna miss her, there's already been too many rings!"

ME: But you didn't miss me. We're talking.

ANN: Shoot. Now I have to run.

For my brother and best friend, Amanda: Please don't answer every phone call with the amount of time you have to talk. "I've only got five. What's up?" Or "What is it. I have two minutes." Or "I can't chat." Then don't answer! Sometimes *they'll* call *me* and immediately announce they only have three minutes to talk. Why call at all!? It's like you're bragging about how little time you have for me!

Don't send texts that imply you have bad news when you don't. Like, "CALL ME AS SOON AS YOU GET THIS." Or "NEED TO TALK TO YOU ASAP." Even a plain "CAN WE TALK?" sends fear through my heart. Please slap a "BUT EVERYTHING'S OKAY!!!" on the end of the text if all you need to tell me is "THERE'S A VIDEO OF SNOOP DOGG JUST SITTING IN HIS CAR AND CRYING, LISTENING TO 'LET IT GO.' HE IS US. JUST THOUGHT YOU SHOULD KNOW." Well, of *course* I need to know that! But put my mind at ease up top so I don't jump off a bridge in anticipation of life-changing despair for no reason. Keep it breezy over text, unless someone else has fallen through a sinkhole.

Try not to fall through a sinkhole.

Don't allow your speaking voice to have an upward inflection when stating a fact. "I'm fine??" "Good to see you??" "I'm going to Bass Lake??" These are statements not questions and it makes you seem dim??

Don't speak too slowly.

The next general "not okay" is when people decide they don't need to play by the rules of society that the rest of us have subscribed to. I'm not talking about the bigger rules, I'm talking about the social contracts we have all figuratively signed. We say "hi" when we walk into a room and are greeted by someone. We smile when smiled at. We respond to an email or text. We RSVP with regrets when not attending a social engagement. If we see someone with a stroller, we hold a door open for them. If we leave a room, we say goodbye. Don't simply decide these rules do not apply to you. These are the bare-ass bones, basics. They apply to you, sweetie! The end.

When replying to an email or a text, we know NEVER to use only these four letters: "OKAY" I find a period at the end of "OKAY." to be even more shattering. Others tell me to take small comfort in the period, but either version is a DEVASTATING response. And when I get a "K"???? A lone "K??" I'm done for the day. I pack it up. You might as well be saying: "I TRULY DESPISE YOU AND WISH YOU EVERY ILL AVAILABLE TO US AS HUMANS. IN FACT, I HOPE YOU END UP RIDDLED TIP TO TUSH WITH AILMENTS SO GRIM, THE NEXT TIME WE COMMUNICATE I'LL FEEL TOO BAD FOR YOU TO EVEN GIVE YOU AN 'OKAY' BUT THAT'S ONLY BECAUSE YOU'LL BE DEAD AND I'LL BE WRITING TO YOUR HUSBAND OR CHILDREN WITH MY CONDOLENCES."

Now, on the opposite end of the spectrum are the responses that are TOO friendly. Too eager to please. Too cheerful. With too many !!!!!!!!, clearly masking murderous rage. Most of the time a simple "Got it thanks!" will do. I myself struggle mightily with this, though recently it's come to my attention that when I over-thank and over-empathize and over-praise and over-give it's not because I am such a nice person, as previously thought, but because I belong in Al-Anon!!!!!

Speaking of murderous rage, here are some quick outlandish "Don'ts" I would be remiss not to mention. While they have all been committed by Real Housewives, I believe they can serve as guidelines for us all. As I've always maintained, we can learn from them:

Don't support your boyfriend in faking cancer (Vicky "OG" Gunvalson).

Don't freeze your dead dog so you can thaw her whenever it suits you to hold her one more time. (Tinsley Mortimer). My friend Shawnta had a great question regarding this behavior: "Is this something white people do?" Apparently it is.

Don't throw your prosthetic leg at people during a dinner party (Aviva Drescher).

Speaking of legs. Don't tell a woman who has just been visiting her aunt in the hospital after the aunt found out she needed dual leg removal surgery, that she needs to get away from you because, quote, "You smell like hospital" (Mary M. Cosby).

Don't spend an entire season asserting you didn't hire a ghostwriter for your novels when you hired a ghostwriter. (You know who.) Although what I would have given if someone had ghostwritten this book, so no judgments there.

Don't attack a cameraman who followed the action of the TV program into your closet, throw him up against the wall, and crack his tooth, requiring his hospitalization (my beloved Ms. Linnethia "NeNe" Leakes).

Don't touch cameramen's bottoms, REPEATEDLY! (Househusband Michael Darby).

Don't say to a fellow housewife: "Your titties are social distancing, bitch" (Porsha Williams). Actually, PLEASE DO, this is a delightful slam.

DON'T TAG ANY of these women. I'm scared of them.

Don't call your friends "baby girl" or call ME "mama." Or use hashtags like #momlyfe or #momofboys or #mamaneedswineamiright!

Don't call a get-together with friends who happen to have children "Moms' Night Out!" We're not just moms, we're more than that! (Similarly, if you have children, not *all* of your necklaces need to feature their initials. Or spell "Mommy" or "Madre" or "Mère" or "Mama.")

Please don't ever ask me, "How's Mom Life treatin' you?" I beg you.

If you're a stay-at-home mom, don't say cheerfully to a working mom when you see her at drop-off, "Haven't seen you around here in forever!" It's an act of terrorism.

If you're a mom who also works outside the home, don't passive-aggressively imply to a stay-at-home mom

that she should feel less than. IF YOU ARE STAYING
HOME WITH KIDS (**I CAN'T DO IT!**) YOU ARE DOING
THE HARDEST WORK OF ALL. THE LORD'S WORK.

Don't, if you're a parent with a partner, complain about
"everything that's on your plate" to a single mom. I amend
the above. THAT is the hardest work.

Don't suddenly decide, in the height of a global pandemic, if you're someone who has never been told by anyone that you're particularly funny, that it's your turn to
step up to the plate and entertain us with comedic Instagram videos, such as ones where you're about to pour
milk into your Cheerios and then last-minute you pour a
bottle of rosé into the bowl instead. We're all set!

Similarly, don't not know if you aren't funny. There is
zero shame in not being funny, only shame in thinking you
are when you're not. (Note: you may not find *me* funny!
And I am prepared to take that fearless feedback.)

Don't last-minute abandon your friend who you were
supposed to take a six-hour cooking class with and send
your husband instead. I don't care to roast a chicken and
make crème brûlée with a guy I say hello to once a year.

Don't say, as the husband of one of my friends did,
when asked on New Year's what his resolution is: "I'd like
to flirt more." (He is the only person I've ever met who
kept his resolution. They are divorced now.)

Do not *not* get Botox just because you have bangs.
One day you'll grow 'em out, and *then* what??

Don't scheme about how you could get your bangs
trimmed through the mail slot in your front door during

the height of the quarantine. (And don't dream of doing the same thing with Botox.)

Don't suggest or demand that groups of people who aren't really friends download an app to stay in touch. Call me an old lady, but I don't need newfangled platforms to not communicate with you.

If you as an adult person engage in couples or family Halloween costumes (which I DO!), please just don't be SO excited by them. Temper yourself.

Don't write gushy open letters to your partner/spouse/ girlfriend or boyfriend on social media extolling their virtues. It's embarrassing.

If you were once a decorated federal prosecutor and are now retired and living next door to me, don't feel it's your job to prosecute our neighborhood. Retire altogether!

Don't be an anti-vaxxer.

Don't be cheap. I often find people with the least are the most generous. Give it away. It will come back.

Don't—this one I have, unfortunately, also learned from experience—under any circumstances suggest to friends struggling with fertility that they "start IVF," "begin the adoption process," "look into surrogacy," "try acupuncture," etc., etc., etc. Information is out there and readily available and it's not your place. It's simply too sensitive.

Don't offer anyone with chronic pain or a critical illness any treatment suggestions based on something you "read." Assume and have respect for the fact they are doing all they can.

Don't complain to a friend who has lost a parent about how annoying your mom is. How many times she wants to visit her grandkids, how smothering she is, how often she wants to talk. . . .

By the same token, don't make others feel as though their problems (however "small" you deem them) aren't as big as yours. It's not cute. No one has a patent on suffering. Assume everyone's pain is deeply real to them. I SAID MANY OF THESE WOULD CONTRADICT EACH OTHER. AND THAT'S BOTH OKAY AND IT'S NOT!!!!!!

Don't clutch your water bottle so smugly. This seems like a small issue, but I'm going somewhere with this! I don't mean this in regards to the environment (love to see everyone with a sustainable bottle). What I object to is the way some women (mostly women, so sorry) clutch their water bottles proudly, bragging about the fact that they drink water throughout the day. WE GET IT! YOU'RE HYDRATED! CONGRATS! The constant clutching feels like a subtle cue you want me to catch that YOU PRACTICE SELF-CARE! YOU VALUE YOUR HEALTH!!! That's great! But not everybody does, so keep it to yourself. And you certainly don't need a jug the size of a tire. It's visually distracting and aggressive.

Please don't drink everything out of a mason jar.

Speaking of. Please don't keep suggesting I practice more self-care. I know you mean well. And I'm all for it as an overall concept, and of course I believe it to be important, especially for women. HOWEVER. Let's all take a step back and calm down. And at least acknowledge that the notion one would even have the luxury/time/money to actively practice self-care is coming from a place of incredible privilege. So let's start there. Now, that said, as someone who has had the means to seek help from every unaccredited guru under the hot Los Angeles sun and who still seems to find the time to steal away for bottom facials, I'm tired of being cheerfully and almost pityingly told, whenever a problem arises, that I just need to "practice more self-care." I'm already leaning in and working full-time while doing 85 percent of the housework, carrying 90 percent of the mental load, and making 79 cents on the dang dollar. Much more disturbing, Black women are making 63 cents, Indigenous women 58 cents, and Latinx women, only 54 cents. And on top of all that, we're supposed to engage in radical self-care? Here's something radical. This is too much to ask of us and from ourselves. Now you'd have me find time to fail at something *else*⁇⁇⁇

How about men step the fuck up and at least attempt to lean in and help us! Could they even try and get in the ballpark of an egalitarian partnership? Women may have been "allowed" to enter the workforce, but it's been a deal with the devil. You can work, but guess what? You'll still do *every single thing* women in the 50s did to keep the inner workings of their homes and families running. You'll just get to work on top of it! Two, three jobs even! There has been one major shift since the 50s and that's the fact that moms today spend TWICE as much time with their kids! So, you'll also get to snowplow-parent your recently facialed, tight bottom off. The other good news is you'll be shamed for taking prescription medication to keep up with it all. (And carry soul-crushing guilt for the rest of your life for what you didn't do.) Once again, I point out how far we haven't come!

Similarly, I'm over this well-meant but rather insufferable demand that we all practice mindfulness all the time. In *these* times?? In *2020*? You want me to be present for *this*?? No thanks! I will be practicing mind*less*ness, please and thank you. Let's all make a pact to live our worst lives.

Don't whistle. My mom used to say, "Avoid whistlers at all costs." I have a very clear memory of standing with my mom at an ATM when we heard whistling coming from a normal-looking guy behind us in line. "Let's go," she said quickly, grabbing my arm. "But how are we going to pay for the Burger King we just ordered and they cooked before we realized we had no money on us??!" We never got the Burger King. She never elaborated on exactly why, but I've tried to steer clear. Except for the man closest to me—my husband—who is a whistler. (But thankfully she hasn't said anything about him because she's dead.) As I've gotten older I think I get why. On a basic level, it's creepy. But beyond that, whistling is basically saying, I am so incredibly at ease in this world I feel fine filling the few sacred silences we have left with the sound of my dippity-doo-dah dipshit whistle. I (don't) hate to generalize but I've noticed that it's usually white men who do this?

Speaking again of white men, if I had a dime for every

time an older white man cut me in line, I'd finally be paid what I'm worth! Now, because I'm a white woman of privilege, I can only imagine women of color experience this 1,000,000 more times often than I do. It's happened so much that I've come to believe that it's not that they see me standing there in line and actively try to cut in front of me. It's actually much darker. They DON'T see me. I'm invisible. I'm a ghost! It's as though their eyeballs cannot see shapes in the forms of female humans.

While we're here, beware the *liberal* white male. We know to shelter in place from conservative white men, but liberal guys are often hiding in plain sight. You could be sleeping with the enemy! The ones who pride themselves on not being part of the problem but rather "part of the solution." Even the most well-meaning, bleeding-heart white men benefit HEALTHILY from the systems of oppression in this country that keep them at the top. And they may allow that boat to be rocked, but they still don't want it tipped over.

And be wary of the liberal white woman. The feminists who I believe are trying very hard to advance women but have often forgotten to include and fight for the advancement of ALL women.

And finally. I know the last dang thing anyone needs is a lecture from a white woman (too late!), so this final "don't" I'll issue to myself (but hope anyone reading this book who identifies as white will join me). Don't assume you aren't racist. You are. I am. Labeling myself racist has been shockingly hard to do. It bursts this bubble we as white people have clung to in order to not have to face the horrors of the past or change the status quo that allows us to benefit. And no well-meaning white person wants to think of themselves as being racist. Because that's a bad thing! We know enough to know we would rather be anything but *that*!

I used to have an utter *meltdown*, a literal explosion of brain, body, and soul, if a friend (generously, I might add) suggested that something I did or said verged on being racist. I COULD. NOT. HANDLE. IT. And I'm really embarrassed about that. And ashamed of that. Of that collapse. That fear.

We have to accept our complicity in this system and have empathy beyond our own experience. And acknowledge the truth. It wasn't just our "hard work" that got us where we are. My grandma and parents paid for my college. In my early twenties my mom sent me money with the earmark "Follow your dreams." My grandfather gave me money I put toward a down payment on my first house. What an unspeakable luxury. We have had a leg up. And had a hand in keeping others down.

What I'm learning on this particular journey—a journey that, if I'm being honest, is much more in its infancy than I thought, is that fear is so boring. And so unproductive.

It stops us from DOING. And that's a don't. See what I did there? (Sorry.)

Gimme Some Sugar; or, The Wreckage of My Presence Redux

I refuse to share treats at the movies. Simply refuse. I like to think I make my policy known in a very up front, yet thoughtful, manner. I simply state to my film-going companion, plainly and evenly, as we stroll up to the concessions:

ME: Oh, hey, really quick—not sure if you already know this about me, but I won't be sharing any of my treats.

At this point the friend usually laughs, assuming I'm joking.

ME: This isn't a drill. I'm quite serious.

FRIEND: Any?

ME: Thank you for asking. By "any" I mean, not a

Vine, not a Goober, not a handful of 'corn, not a sip of Dr Pep, not a Cinnabite. NOTHING. However—

FRIEND: Not even *one* bite?!?!

ME: One bite, in my mind, may as well be the whole thing. That's what I'm trying to impress upon you. Even though the bag of Reese's Pieces seems big enough to share, I'm asking you to expand your consciousness and understand that for me, one thousand Pieces isn't enough.

Typically, the friend has his or her mouth open in shock and tries to bypass my vehemence:

FRIEND: I'm fine, I don't even want anything.

ME: Right *now*. Right now you think you don't want anything. And that is why I am going to buy you exact replicas of what I'm ordering, on the off, off chance that once we get in there and the lights lower, the mood suddenly strikes and you'll be all set and won't come crying to me.

FRIEND *(annoyed)*: I'm *telling* you, I don't want anything. Sheesh.

ME: That's what they all say. But I've been through this enough times to know that when you hear me rattling my wrappers and slurping away, you may be singin' a different tune. And I don't want you to get

caught with your pants down. Because as much as I
hate having to say this to you, whom I consider a close
friend, once again, my position will remain the same. I
will not be sharing.

We let a couple move past us in line.

FRIEND: This is insane. I'm not going to let you pay for
snacks I'm not going to eat—

ME: If you don't end up eating them, WONDERFUL!
Hats off. But I'll be safe in there, knowing you aren't
comin' a knockin'. Because if I can't enjoy the movie
and these concessions freely, I'm at an emotional deficit,
and quite frankly, I'm afraid of what might happen.

FRIEND: I'm truly stunned and deeply saddened for you.

We are now at the register.

CONCESSION WORKER: Welcome to the Arclight. What can
I get you?

ME *(brightly)*: We'll take two hot dogs, two Milk Duds,
two Red Vines, two large popcorns no butter, two large
Dr Peppers and . . . I think that's good. For now.

I DIDN'T FIND this out until years later, but apparently
when I gave that lil speech to my sister-in-law, she went

home, called her best friend, and said, "My brother is dating a selfish psychopath."

And here I thought this routine had the same kind of lovable quirkiness as Zooey Deschanel's bangs and glasses. Turns out, in both cases, people were over it.

No, I never thought I had a problem with sugar. Until this year, when I realized not only did I have a problem, but I also had a full-blown sugar addiction.

The signs had all been there. Hadn't they?

Wasn't I the toddler whose parents would have to tell every baby-sitter not to say the word *C-O-O-K-I-E* in front of me, or else I wouldn't stop begging and crying to have one? (One sitter f'ed up and told me I was "one smart cookie" and paid dearly. Though I sincerely appreciated the compliment.)

Wasn't it me who at age seven knocked her front teeth out on the kitchen counter jumping up and down, losing my mind with excitement, as I waited for my grandpa to pour me another glass of grape juice?

And wasn't it me who would take the occasional twenty-dollar bill my grandpa would send and IMMEDIATELY announce to whoever my two besties were that day that we were getting off the bus one stop early so I could treat everyone to as much candy as it could buy us at The Little Green Store? We would lay out our bounty on the concrete of the public tennis court next door. 5th Avenue Bars. Butterfingers. Big League Chew by the handfuls. Reese's Cups. Six feet of Bubble Tape I would consume in one serving. Cherry Cokes, Hostess mini

chocolate-covered donuts, the ones where the taste is so
purely manufactured and man-made they are a work of
art. Long after my friends would tire of the candy or feel
sick from it, I forged ahead. A pioneer.

I would hide half-eaten bowls of Honey Nut Cheerios
on the top shelf of my closet. They'd get buried among
school papers and Trapper Keepers and notebooks. This
was most likely because of laziness, rather than a need to
hide my consumption, but I have always had a shadowy
sense that I liked sugar in a way and in quantities that
were not normal.

In seventh-grade orchestra, we had to sell candy to
raise money for our rinky-dink field trips to Crystal City,
an underground shopping nightmare where we would
sing Christmas carols and pray a natural disaster didn't
seal us into its tunnels. I was my only and best customer.
I would eat all the Kit Kats, the Nestlé Crunch bars, and
my favorite, the all-purple Mike and Ikes. They tasted as
if God Himself had taken an honest appraisal of what humans, especially twelve-year-old girls, would really want
in a candy and created one so oblong, so stale, so grapey,
so sugary, you had no choice but to fall to your knees and
thank Him (or Her).

The Girl Scouts were also lucky to have me. My best
friend, Amanda, and I would set out to sell cookies in
the August heat and, after knocking on three doors, decide we'd better call it a day. We'd park ourselves on our
church steps or head to the bench by the tennis courts and
dig in, downing SLEEVES of Thin Mints and boxes of

Tagalongs. We avoided the Samoas, as any sane people would, gave the "new flavor" a fighting chance, and even settled for some Trefoils if we were desperate enough. As our slogan said, "A Girl Scout is willing to help out wherever she is needed." We were doing our part.

When it was time to *pay* for the cookies I would be thrown into a blind panic and either steal money from my eight-year-old brother, or dig up the ten-dollar bill Amanda and I had recently buried in the backyard in a "treasure chest," promising never to dig it up, ever, or at least not for fifty years. Mostly, though, I would call my grandpa.

"How much do you need, Sug?" Grandpa Red called me Sugar, so he clearly shoulders some of the blame. "Well," I would say, twisting the phone cord around the corner of the kitchen into our minuscule mudroom and lowering my voice. "Probably like, um, about a hundred and seventy-five dollars?" "WHAT?!?!" he'd yell back into the phone. I would be sweating. "I'll pay you back, I promise!! At some point . . . please don't tell my mom!"

Even though it may seem like Grandpa Red's enabling was part of the problem, he was actually the solution. He was a shelter in the storm. He made sure I had the soft landing I needed in the in-between times when my mom would go in her bedroom and close the door for a weekend. Or during the week-long business trips my dad would have to take and my mom's mood would turn "blue," as she called it. Even though he lived thousands of miles away, my grandpa made sure that I had a friend with me at all times. Candy. She was always with me during the fearful times, the lonely times. The uncertain moments, the days when the puzzle pieces were not to be found.

Whenever our family would make our annual pilgrimage to Florida, my grandma baked chocolate chip cookies so crispy you could scream. She would stack them neatly in Tupperware containers, and one would be set out for me with four more in the freezer, next to her lasagnas and sausages and peppers, all made from scratch. My heart would race as we pulled into their driveway from the airport. I would sprint through their garage, throw down my bags, and attack the cookies. And then there was the cupboard. "What can we get for you, Sug?" my grandpa would call to ask in his gentle drawl about a week out from our departure. He knew me enough to know my obsessions were subject to change. And when I arrived, it was like Christmas in August, with a Costco-size pack of peanut butter M&M's waiting in the pantry with my name on it. Twelve bags! All for me. Twelve bags of love.

To this day, I OFTEN tear up at the sight of a bag of peanut butter M&M's. Because my grandpa and sweets were the heart and the soul of my childhood, and they are almost interchangeable in my mind. Both a warm blanket. Both my dear pals who were always there and always looked out for me.

And up until a year ago, candy and I remained joined at the hip. Frenemies, though, really. I enjoyed hanging out less and less, and felt sick and demoralized after our times together, but I couldn't quit her.

I sought help to gain the courage to break up at every turn. Well-meaning nutritionists/trainers/friends/ anorexics would offer the same type of advice, advice normal eaters could follow without a problem.

But I wasn't a normal eater. And I had heard it all before. "Maybe try not having Justin's peanut butter cups for like, a week, see if you even miss them . . . I bet you won't!" Or: "It takes thirty days to break a habit. So just commit to thirty days without sugar. That's NOTHING. Think about how short that actually is in the scheme of life. . . ."

I would stare back at whoever was saying this with total disdain. And try and gather myself. Praying I could keep a lid on the well of rage rocketing through my body. Holding back what the little girl inside me was screaming: DON'T YOU THINK I'VE FUCKING TRIED THAT?????????!!!!!!!!! IF I COULD I WOULD!!

But I could not. Truly. It wasn't a matter of willpower. The will was there. But it was like asking someone who had never climbed a flight of stairs to "give Everest a try. On your own. We'll meet you at the summit. And do it for thirty days."

As my career progressed, I would seek out increasingly expensive nutritionists who hawked harder-core, even more restrictive plans to fit the entitled clientele they served. It was like the closer to Beverly Hills their offices were, the more they needed to flog and dominate us. The regimen was always the same: cut out sugar, dairy, and

carbs and have a great one! Well, no doy, you ding dong
dang idiots. I knew *what* to do but I was in search of *how*
to do it.

And so, each new nutritionist brought with him or her
the promise that they would be the one to finally help me
figure it out. It was the same routine, give or take, every
time. I would listen attentively to my new plan, take my
personalized handout (where "tropical fruit" had always
been aggressively crossed out), and pore over the results
of my In Body Fit Test or blood test or oxygen test with
growing resolve. This was gonna be the one! But just as
the clinician was about to send me on my way with my
marching orders, I always had one more tiny little question. One that never garnered the answer I wanted.

ME: Um, so this is all great stuff. And I'm looking
forward to it. But um, what about on, say, like,
Thursday night—what do I do then?

NUTRITIONIST: Thursday night?

ME: Right. Thursday night is sort of, historically,
when the wheels come off and things like this
(gesturing to my sheet) . . . fall away. Like on Monday
I'm flying high, feeling sorry for everyone who
can't diet like I can, the fat fucks who don't want
to prioritize their health . . . then Tuesday is like,
okay, this is a tad harder but I'm still on my way
to a fantastic life beyond my wildest dreams and

Wednesday is like, "Huh." And then by Thursday
around seven P.M. it's like, "Uh-oh. Me want candy.
Me want food. Me want it now." Then Friday
morning is a last-ditch effort to salvage things but
by four P.M. it's a shit show and then Saturday is a
descent into hell and by Sunday I am eating every
tier in my bag of Pepperidge Farm Mint Milanos. I'm
ordering pizza and cinnamon sticks and hiding some
of them from dinner guests on the off chance there is
another little piggy like me in attendance. Then they
leave and I binge TV and mainline candy until I pass
out in a food coma and wake up as angry a human as
you'll ever see and by Monday morning I'm googling
new diets because yours didn't work and I am so
disgusted with myself I have no choice but to start
alllll over again. And repeat. For the last twenty-five
years or so.

The nutritionist will now give me a series of long
blinks. But shockingly won't be deterred.

NUTRITIONIST: Okay. That was a lot . . . BUT—

I know what's coming. It's the same every time. Swap-
outs. Less flavorful options for the thing you want most,
which ends up driving you to that very thing even faster.
Tips and tricks to quiet the obsession. Presented all the
while with well-meaning, perky motherfucking smiles on
their faces.

NUTRITIONIST: What *if?????* Instead of all that candy, when the urges hit on Thursday, what if you had, for instance, INSTEAD . . . a cozy cup of mint tea?

This is followed by a soul-crushing silence while I process how a human who has just heard another human discuss the hellscape of her unhealthy relationship to food and disassociation from herself could not understand that a cup of fucking mint tea ain't gonna cut it. It ain't even gonna scratch the goddamn surface, you thin entitled basic white bitch.

ME: Well, if that's my option, I assure you I will fail.

NUTRITIONIST: A nibble of ninety-eight percent cacao dark chocolate???

I stand up and quietly gather my things.

NUTRITIONIST: Some watermelon slices with a dash of sea salt???

I take out my wallet, readying myself for the reception desk.

ME: Thanks, but I have been trying to express to you . . . I need SOMETHING. Something to hold on to, to hang my hat on, to be the light at the end of a hard day. So, if you aren't willing to offer me diddly shit, I cannot do this program.

I start walking out, and she follows me.

NUTRITIONIST: It's just, well, you said you wanted to lose weight . . .

ME: Not that badly!

NUTRITIONIST: Okay, what about . . . what about . . . a Halloween-size snack pack of M&M's . . .

ME *(turning back)*: Listening . . .

NUTRITIONIST: Twice a week . . .

I keep walking.

NUTRITIONIST: Three times a week? Four?? I mean I really want you to succeed here but, okay, what if, okay wait—what if you can have one of those every night?? As a treat? The weight loss will be slower but . . .

I turn and look at her and give her my final offer.

ME: Three snack-size bags of M&M's each weeknight, and weekends are a choose-your-own adventure. Those are my terms. Take them or leave them.

I extend my hand. The nutritionist is deeply confused, because I came here to get advice, not bargain someone down to cosigning a nondiet. But she wants her $350, and so she extends her hand and we shake.

ME *(smiling)*: See you next Wednesday!

But we both know I won't see her next Wednesday. By the following Wednesday, that woman will be the proud new owner of my $2,000 package of ten sessions. I will not be back. I will have blown more money than I have in the bank begging someone to tell me how to eat and be healthy like an adult woman ought to, and then promptly failed. And it's happened over and over and over and over and over again.

Most likely it's because it was in my blood. My mom took me to my first Weight Watchers meeting when I was home from NYU for Thanksgiving. We laughed until we cried. Literally, tears streamed down our faces as we were handed paper plates with nothing on them and told we were going to do a "dry run" of Thanksgiving. It was more embarrassing than anything I'd done in acting class, pretending to shuffle through an invisible buffet with a group of well-meaning guys and gals. Bless them, everyone except my mom and I took "small portions" and then sat down and ate their IMAGINARY food, slowly and thoughtfully. Even though there was no real food, my mom said she wanted to go back up for seconds. We could not stop laughing. Not wanting to make anyone feel bad, we hurried out so we could be free to howl with laughter in the car. When my mom reversed, she caught a golden arch in her rearview and stepped on it. We were pulling into the McDonald's drive-thru before some of the ladies had gotten their shoes back on after weigh-in. Laughing all the way. We really showed them.

But we didn't actually show them. Neither of us. After my mom's sudden heart attack at age fifty-four, I met with a cardiologist to understand my own odds. Could it have been the number of Cokes she drank daily? (Six.) Could it have been all her binges and sugar? Not exercising beyond leisurely strolls around the neighborhood with friends and signing up for seven hundred YMCA memberships she never used? He told me it was probably none of those things—that for a woman to suffer a fatal heart attack at fifty-four was simply a terrible twist of fate. A .000001 percent chance freak occurrence. So, I left it there. Despite seeing the word *obesity* listed on her death certificate under "cause." Which was one of the saddest things I have ever seen. To reduce someone's life to one cruel word broke my heart. Especially someone who cared deeply about their appearance.

Twelve years later, I was five months into my second pregnancy and was driving across town when I got a call out of the blue from my dad. I was feeling pretty down that day. Partly because I felt nauseous all the time. Partly because the baby had a heart murmur, which was thankfully totally innocuous but meant I was forced to go cold turkey off my daily cup of coffee. But MAINLY I was depressed because I couldn't stop eating junk food. Not the way women you can't even tell are pregnant from behind love to say merrily, "I'm giving in to my cravings! If I want ice cream after dinner I have ice cream! I'm being *bad*!" In my normal life I "gave in" quite a bit but I had a handle on things. I wouldn't eat sugar during the day because it has the same effect on my body chemistry as alcohol does on alcoholics. I crave sugar desperately but then when I eat it I feel terrible and angry, which leads me to act out and then pass out. And now that I was pregnant and feeling sick all the time my normal defenses were down and I Could. Not. Stop. Eating. Candy. And more candy and any treats and sweets I could get my little paws on. I was in a sugary hell spiral.

When a doctor told me I needed to pull back, I wailed in the parking garage to my husband. I wanted to pull back. I never *didn't want* to pull back. But I couldn't pull back. It was impossible. Because, I realized, I am a compulsive sugar addict.

And so it was in the midst of this internal battle, alone in my car, that my dad told me he wanted to tell me something. "Enough time has passed," he said. Has it ever been enough time to hear bad news? I braced myself. He told me that as much as it pained him to say, he believed my mom's heart attack had been brought on after years and years of Ritalin abuse and addiction. It was a drug she initially took to keep her weight down. And later kept taking to have the energy required to raise two kids with a husband constantly on the road, work full-time as a beloved preschool director, all the while volunteering at our church and leading practically every PTA committee and showing up for every event Fletcher and I ever had ever. Apparently, I suddenly realized, you don't get the nickname "Kathy I'll Do Anything for My Daughter" Wilson without pharmaceutical help. . . .

I pulled over on the side of Beverly Boulevard and did a quick Google search. A search that illuminated my entire childhood. In two seconds every question I have ever had, not only about my mom but also about me, my childhood, incidents that shall not be written about, were answered. I finally had the missing piece. Side effects of Ritalin abuse include: anger, agitation, insomnia, paranoia, panic attacks, suspicion, aggression, psychosis, crashing, low appetite followed by exceptional hunger, irritability, depression, mood swings, and fatigue. The last "side effect" took my breath away. Prolonged use may cause sudden heart attack.

The puzzle was complete. Ritalin withdrawal was what I was seeing when my mom would hole up once a month and not emerge for a full weekend. Her addiction explained why she would often still be awake at 3:00 A.M., hammering away on a new DIY project or decorating cubbies for her preschoolers. Or why she was sometimes still in a nightgown at 3:00 P.M. And why she barely ever ate and then would binge on incomprehensible amounts of junk food. And why her mood swings could be so wild and out of control. And why she couldn't contain her anger. Or sadness. Or joy. And why we never knew what we were going to get. We had been at the mercy of a terrible drug in the methamphetamine category. And so had she.

My dad told me she had tried and succeeded many times over the years to get off of it. But then she would start taking it again. In the last couple of years, he truly thought she had stopped for good, but when he was packing up her things in the hotel room she had died in on their vacation, he found three pills in her quilted red change purse. My dad explained he hadn't told Fletcher or me at the time because he didn't want that news to interfere with our grieving process or our opinion of our mom. Because he, too, didn't want my mom reduced to one word. "She was," he said, his voice breaking, "a terrific, loving, talented, funny, gorgeous, life-loving woman who was trying her best. And who succeeded at more than most people will in their entire lives. And I hope you remember her this way." He was only telling us because it occurred to him that we were now parents and that we needed to be extremely careful, that addiction runs in the family. And because I'd mentioned once that I'd used diet pills (phentermine) to lose baby weight after Max and was fully planning on doing it again after baby number two. And he was calling to plead with me not to. My mind flashed back to the week I'd abruptly stopped taking them. It had been one of the darker weeks of my life, even by the standards of the postpartum low I'd been in, and I couldn't figure out why it was *that* bad. Finally, I put together that even though I had only taken the pills for a month, I'd been detoxing. And it was not pretty. My heart swelled with compassion for my mom.

My hands were shaking, but a strange sense of calm was washing over my whole body. I felt deep relief. To know, finally. To have finally gotten the answer to a question no one else ever seemed to be asking.

I told my dad I was really grateful that he had waited until now to tell me. This, after all, is the man who had group texted the following an hour prior:

RACHEL OSLO. DEAD. FUNERAL SUNDAY. I HEARD THEY
CAN'T DO OPEN CASKET! TRYING TO FIGURE OUT WHY.
STAY TUNED!!!

Only one person responded:

HI PAUL, THIS IS DUSTIN YOUR LANDSCAPER. I THINK YOU
MEANT TO TEXT THIS TO SOMEONE ELSE.

But my dad handled this so beautifully. I couldn't have processed this revelation a second earlier. Certainly not right after she died, when I was drifting through the middle place—between life at home as a child and life with a partner. And now that I'm a mom, I told him (and on this I could not be more clear), I don't blame her at all. Not one single solitary bit. I understood her as deeply and fully as I ever have. It was *not* knowing the answers that kept a wall between us.

What I long to be able to tell her (and have expressed through prayer and meditation and honestly through this book—here's hoping she reads it) is this:

Mommy,

It's so fine. It's so very fine to want to be better. To look better. To do better. To feel overwhelmed. To feel self-conscious. To feel trapped. To not know how to get out of something. Or be able to when you do know. Life is so hard. It's okay to want to soften the edges. You were brave. You put yourself out there. You worked so hard to create change, and that takes a toll. You gave us so much. You had such a generous heart, so many big feelings (like me) and I understand. I get it. I'm mainly just so sorry you were ever suffering. I wish you got the help I am able to get. But it was a different time. And it's okay. You were just being human. A warrior. A lioness. A Mama Bear. A big-hearted dynamo named Kathy Wilson, trying to do it all. And you are so much more than this. I love you to pieces.

Love,

Casey Rose

A LITTLE OVER a year ago, I decided the only way to honor her struggle is by making better choices for myself. I finally felt ready. Ready as I'd ever be to attend my first 12-step meeting, for food addiction. The same program my old boss, Barbara, had so inappropriately demanded I try sixteen years earlier. Walking into that meeting room was one of the most uncomfortable things I have *ever* done. Later, someone told me, it's also one of the most courageous, because as 12-step programs go, it's in some ways the least socially acceptable one. Weight discrimination is still so pervasive in our culture. I mean, Alcoholics

Anonymous is like, "At least I'm fun!" Narcotics Anonymous is, "Sue me, I like to party!" Al-Anon is all, "It's not *my* fault!" and then you have the food program, which is just, "I CAN'T STOP EATING!!!!"

I felt physically ill in the meetings for the first few weeks. I was turned off by the vulnerability and struggled mightily with acceptance that this was indeed a real problem, and one I could not control on my own. Thankfully, with the help of an incredible sponsor, I was drawn back in by the promise that maybe, just maybe, there was an answer out there. Not an answer for my weight—I was so beyond interested in even losing weight. I was fine with my weight. But my inner monologue surrounding sugar and what I was eating was so toxic I reached a breaking point. I have a beautiful life beyond my wildest dreams. I wanted to enjoy it. And I was actually in a place where I felt strong enough to tackle this, the thing that had plagued me since the day I was born. I've been able to do a lot in my life, but my sugar compulsion has been the one thing I could never seem to get ahold of. And I was tired of beating myself up over it. I felt ready— and had nowhere else to go. I couldn't do another diet if I tried. I was ready to lay down my sword.

As I delved in, I was surprised to learn that it wasn't a dieting program. It's a spiritual program. I have a problem, a disease actually, one I have been failing miserably to control because I CAN'T control my addiction to sugar. It was counterintuitive. All this time I'd felt there was something so helplessly wrong with me. But all along, that was the answer. I can't. And the program is based around the admission of that fact, acknowledging that I am powerless over it, and turning it over to a power greater than me. IT'S GOD'S PROBLEM NOW, MOTHERFUCKERS! And something in the surrendering, as anyone who has worked a 12-step program knows, is so freeing—it's like a weight comes off of you (pun intended). There is peace in knowing you *can't* do anything. For an ambitious perfectionist, this is both revolutionary and excruciating. But what a goddamn relief. Joining was so humbling and terrifying, but that was actually the hardest part. It's being taken care of for me. I actually have to do very little. And the miracles I had been exhorted to expect, way back when in that Marianne Williamson seminar, have begun to unfold in even greater scope than they had been. Simple miracles. Or maybe I'm just able to see them now.

I'm tired of viewing myself as a failure. And I don't view anyone who struggles with addiction or depression or anxiety or mental illness as a failure. And so, I'm *attempting* to move forward with complete empathy and compassion for myself, the same empathy and compassion I extend to my mom. It's slow going, for sure, but something has been lifted. My obsession with sugar will always be with me, but I've been able, for today at least, to put our friendship on hold.

At the end of my first meeting, as everyone stood up to leave, the leader for the week issued an edict that has never left me. He gestured to the empty coffee cups and water bottles on the floor next to our seats and said

INCREDIBLY casually, over his shoulder, almost as an afterthought, "Hey, guys. Don't forget to take the wreckage of your presence."

The wreckage of my presence. The wreckage of my presence.

How could I forget?

ACKNOWLEDGMENTS

I am brimming with gratitude for everyone who helped me with this book. And because it is a collection of stories from my life, I must thank the people who have supported me, loved me, picked me up, and cheered me on through the wreckage. . . .

To my book agent, the incomparable David Kuhn. Thank you for your eye, your savvy, and your Housewives gossip. Nate Muscato, you have been endlessly sweet and helpful.

To my editor, Emily Griffin. I always wanted to have "an editor" because I liked the way it sounded, but you have been more than I ever could have imagined. You are brilliant, thoughtful, and kind. I breathlessly await YOUR book!

Thank you to everyone at HarperCollins: Caroline Johnson for the beautiful cover of my dreams; Jonathan Burnham, Doug Jones, Tina Andreadis, Leah Wasielewski, Katie O'Callaghan, and Rachel Elinsky for their publishing vision. Shelly Perron for her copyediting genius. And Andrew Jacobs for the legal expertise.

There are so many VISIONARIES who have believed in me over the years, but I must say a very special thank-you to the following people: Meg Mortimer, Jodi Peikoff, Jennifer

Silver, Marissa Devins, Dan Erliq, Naomi Odenkirk, Brooke Pobjoy, Sarah Clossey, Jo Yao, Logan Eisenberg, Rachel Arlook, Jackie Knobbe, and the United Talent Agency. Steve and Ruth Kirsch, Jeff Obermiller, Heidi Rose Robbins, Heidi Sherman Grey, Julie Yorn, Alan and Peter Rich, Kate Hudson, Anne Hathaway, P. J. Shapiro, Brian Lazarus, Jeff Wolman, Yolanda Romo, Derek Waters, Scott Aukerman, Jordan Cahan, Paul Scheer, Bob Odenkirk, Jonathan Groff, Gail Lerner, the Russo Brothers, Heather Rae, Dori Sperko, Adam Silver, Demi Moore, Sherry Thomas, Lindsay Shookus, Andy Cohen, Lorne Michaels, Jessica Elbaum, David Fincher, Nora Ephron, and Christopher Guest.

And to our dearest Jamie Tarses. You were a force. A trailblazer. A lioness. And above all, a sweetheart. Thank you for everything.

Michelle Margolis and Alexandra Crotin, my hardworking, fun, and NORMAL publicists.

Kim Cooper, April Mouton, Rosa Campos, and Sayra Lemus for your incalculable and invaluable help. It's so appreciated.

My longtime makeup artist and friend, Kathleen Karridene. You are the G.O.A.T (even though I've given you *such* a beautiful canvas to work from).

The Jane Club and its members, who inspire me daily.

The delightful listeners of *Bitch Sesh*. Thank you for wading into the garbage with me and for your immense generosity. You get it!

Dr. Scott Cohen of Beverly Hills Pediatrics.

My beloved high school drama teacher, Flo West. T.C. Williams High School. My brilliant college acting teacher, Lisa Benavides. Tom Oppenheim and every teacher at the Stella

Adler Studio of Acting. Owen Burke and the Upright Citizens Brigade Theatre. Earwolf. My beauties from DPhiE. My girls from Girl Scout Troop 1368. Our savior C.R.P.S. And Commonwealth Baptist Church.

My godparents, Bob and Gretchen Dudney, the Dawkins family, Carolyn Beckett-Coppelman, the Crooks (who only stole my heart)! My sweet kindergarten teacher, Karen Mitsoff, you are so missed. As are you, Jeff Gustafson.

Laura Lynne Jackson.

Jennifer Harkins, for making it all possible. Thank you for caring for my boys in the extraordinary way that you do.

My manager, friend, and spectacular human being, Christie Smith. Constant contact.

Dr. Hattie Beth Myers. Words simply fail. (But thanks for listening to so many of mine.)

The late, great Reverend Nancy Foil.

To my lovely mom friends, who have lifted me up on this complex, beautiful journey.

The Mutt Mafia: "Echuddy!!!"

My beloved A.V. Club since third grade: Meg, Cala, Colleen, Liz, and Petra.

My dearest of touchstones: Deanna, Blair, Kevin, Whitney, Lindy, Courtney, Jessi, Clare, Adam, Zoe, Jessica, Shawnta, Morgan, Paul, and Paul.

Danielle Schneider. Never has a kinder, funnier person walked the earth.

My Coeur: Laura, Patrizia, Matt, and Kulap. I wouldn't be here without you.

June Diane Raphael. My partner in crime. My North Star. You say, "One should never trust a woman with three names," and yet . . . I trust you more than anyone.

Dianne "Queen" Childers. Love you so.

Dr. Amanda Sovik-Johnston. My sister. Thanks for still taking baths with me.

Grandpa Pink, Grandpa Red, Grandma Louise, and Grandma Rita. I was so lucky to have you all in my life for the time that I had you. Until we meet again.

Uncle Alan, taken much too soon, who helped mold everything from my sense of humor to my love of Bette Davis and *Little Shop of Horrors*. Not a day goes by.

My ceaselessly supportive family:

My New York soft landing, Bruce, Carol, and Sophia. The great Jimmy Jet. My treasured aunts and uncles, Ann and Ralph and Bruce and Sharon, who have loved me like a daughter. My cuz-bro, Brian. My beloved Naomi (MoMo) and Jeffrey (BaBa), I hit the in-law jackpot! My adored bonus sisters and brother, Kathleen, Shira, and Buncle T. My stepmom, Marjorie (MiMi). I love you and thank you for loving my kids so deeply.

My everythings: Emma, Clementine, and Teddy.

My brother, Fletcher. "Though I've grown old, the bell still rings for me, as it does for all who truly believe."

The man, the myth, my Daddio, Paul Wilson. You are the most generous person I have ever met. *(sung)* "He's a great dad. He deserves a nap, Dad!"

My mama, Kathy Wilson. I'm so happy our conversation has continued. "Farther Along we'll know all about it. Farther Along we'll understand why . . ."

David. Simply put, you are the best thing that ever happened to me. "In spite of ourselves, we'll end up a-sittin' on a rainbow . . ."

My angels on earth, Max Red and Henry Bear. I love you to pieces.

ABOUT THE AUTHOR

Casey Wilson is an actress, writer, director, and podcaster. Her TV acting credits include *Happy Endings, Saturday Night Live, Easy Mark, Marry Me, Black Monday, Mrs. Fletcher,* and *Curb Your Enthusiasm.* Her film credits include *Gone Girl, Julie & Julia,* and *Always Be My Maybe.* Casey cowrote and costarred in the movies *Bride Wars* and *Ass Backwards* with her longtime collaborator June Diane Raphael.

Alongside Danielle Schneider, she cohosts the hit podcast *Bitch Sesh.* Her directorial debut, *Daddio,* premiered at SXSW and TIFF.

Casey lives with her husband and two young sons in Los Angeles.